CUZ

Thank you!
Stay wonderful!
God Bless!
Cousin Lucy
1/04

Mother's Day
May 9, 2004
from
Jan

CUZ

CUZ ©Copyright 2003
Doris Freeman & Cindie Haynie

Cover Design and Art by Cindie Haynie and Annette Galloway

Put Your Shoes on © 1964 - Sallie Louise McCaskill
T-E-N-N-E-S-S-E-E Spells Heaven to Me © 1953 - Kay Twomey, Tony Starr, and Fred Wise
Uncle Fud©July 1958 - Allan Rankin Jones & Dorothy Shay

All rights reserved.
Printed and bound in the United States of America. Except as permitted under the U.S. Copyright Act of 1976, no part of this may be reproduced or distributed in any form or stored in a data base or retrieval system without prior written permission from the publisher or author.

First Edition September 2003
Library of Congress Cataloguing Number 536 545

ISBN # 0-9741294-7-X

Published by Main Street Publishing Inc., Jackson, Tennessee. Printed and bound by NetPub Corp., Poughkeepsie, New York. Edited by Cindie Haynie. Copy editing by Annette W. Galloway. For information write to Main Street Publishing Inc., 206 East Main Street, Suite 207, P.O. Box 696, Jackson, Tn 38302. E-mail MSP at words@mspbooks.com. Phone: 1-800-224-7649. Visit us at www:mainstreetpublishing.com.

Cuz

"Tuning in with Cousin Tuny"

Written by
Doris Freeman
in cahoots with
Cindie Haynie

Main Street Publishing, Inc.   Jackson, Tn

CUZ

All of this might be fact.

If you ain't in here,
play like you are.

Names have been changed
to protect the guilty…
guilty of love,
guilty of fun,
guilty of trying to
fulfill a life.

CUZ

ACKNOWLEDGMENTS

It is impossible to acknowledge everyone who has been so loyal, loving, helpful, faithful and supportive, but I must recognize some of them. My fabulous four children, Pat, Cindie, Jim, and Connie, always my number one priority; my gorgeous four grandsons, Stephen, Brad, Jay, and Ben; my beautiful great grandson, Jack and the second one we are expecting, and all their families; my extended family, Stan and Chris Harris and their families.

A super special kudo to my daughter, Cindie Haynie, for really putting this book together and making it happen. You are fantastic!

To the precious memories of my family that have passed on and of the love of my life, Bill (W.C.) Harris.

Kudos to our publisher dn, and Annette along with all the Main Street Publishing Staff.

And last but certainly not least, kudos to "you"... all you wonderful people who have touched my life and made it better.

When I count my blessings, I count you twice. Thank you for being you! I love you all.

God bless,
Cuz

CUZ

FOREWORD

Throughout life, most of us have been fortunate to have known people who, at the mention of their names, bring a smile upon our faces. People who constantly focus on giving when giving was sometimes hard to do. A person who never hesitates when a volunteer is asked to step forward. A person who would totally sacrifice their wants to serve others. You who are reading this have probably got an image in your mind of such a person. When I think of people that fit in the category, I automatically think of Doris (Cousin Tuny) Freeman.

My first remembrance of Cousin Tuny was back in the late 1950's. At that time, she was the host of a television program where she was surrounded by adoring kids. It was every child's wish, back in those days, to celebrate their birthday with their friends and Cousin Tuny. With Sealtest milk, hot dogs, cake and ice cream, the joy and happiness we each shared left a loving memory to cherish all of our days.

For many years, my dad, Carl Perkins, and Cousin Tuny worked together on both the Cerebral Palsy and Child Abuse Telethons. They were a team, partners to the heart, who saw the need and rose to the task. After each telethon, they would both be physically and emotionally drained, but never a complaint. For their blessing came in knowing that a child's life would hopefully be for the better.

I truly believe that the Good Lord has angels walking among us. Angels who exemplify what God wants each of us to be like. Total unselfishness, unconditional love, tireless giving to others. We who know her realize that Cousin Tuny fits this definition. Those of you who do not know her can experience this great lady in this book. I ask you before you start reading, to open up your heart and experience the blessing that you will receive as you read the life of Doris (Cousin Tuny) Freeman.

Stan Perkins

PROLOGUE

"Pritchett"

As my memory goes back, backward oh backward turn time in your flight, make me a child again just for tonight...

Daddy was an old Vaudeville hoofer... one of the greatest buck-and-wing dancers in the business. He used to dance on top of the boxcars, coming into town, when he worked on the freight trains. Preening in his uniform, he'd put that rosebud on, and say "Oh God, the women, they're gonna love me this trip!" (Real backward and shy kid, like his children.)

Anyway, I danced before I walked. My father would pick me up and set me on the counter of the Illinois Central Railroad Restaurant where all the railroad men hung out. I'd tap-tap-tap from one end of the bar to the other while they threw pennies on the shiny bar top. I laughed and stared at the spinning copper in awe.

We'd get on the front porch on Sunday and Daddy used to say "Come on, Pritchett." He called me Pritchett 'cause it was this little girl's name who lived alongside the railroad tracks, and he said she looked just like me.

Now, my Sunday-go-to-meetin' wardrobe was somethin' to behold, folks, at least in my eyes: a silk pongee dress... rosette ribbons on my shoulders, the streamers of ribbons hanging down to the top of the hem; smocking all around. The yoke was smocked in pale multi-colors, little puffed sleeves; and it gathered and hung straight to just above my knees, with bloomers that matched. Gold beauty pins on my shoulders kept my little slips

CUZ

with wide straps up (they called them Gertrudes back then)... along with hard-heeled patent leather slippers with buckles on top and socks to match the dress...

I'd go in and my father would say "All right, say your piece now, Pritchett."

I'd say, pointing to my shoulders, "Roses on my shoulders, Slippers on my feet, I'm Daddy's little darlin', Don't you think I'm sweet."

Daddy'd just applaud and say "Come over here and give me some sugar."

And we'd head out to the front porch. (Mother wouldn't let us dance inside, we'd mess up the hardwood floors.)

As Chairman of the Board of Deacons in the old Second Baptist Church here in Jackson, Tennessee, Daddy held prayer meeting and knew the Bible from cover to cover. Some of the good Baptist sisters saw us on the front porch, out there goin'-like-a-train, dancing.

The Board of Deacons held a meeting and told him that it was sinful. They continued, "Now if you will get up in front of the congregation and make a pledge that you will never dance again and you will not allow your daughter to dance, then you can remain active in this church."

He said "Yes, I do want to get up in front of the church."

'Course, as Daddy told it, the older he got... I can see him rared back now with a glass of beer in one hand and a cigar in the other hand -- the story got bigger and bigger and bigger. He made it more interesting; said it was the greatest performance he'd ever done.

There wasn't even standing room that night in the church. He stood in the pulpit and orated: "Now, Brethren, I am here tonight on account of bein' called up in front of the Board of Deacons because me and my baby girl dance. And I am told that if I continue to do this, you all say I will go to hell and my baby girl will go to hell and you'll throw me out of the church. I came to tell you this. You know, all of you adulterers and all of you sinners and all of you long-forked tongue women and men in this church, you better beware, because God laid His hand on my baby girl and me -- and that talent is a talent that's God-given. Now when I die, I am going to heaven and I'm gonna dance right down the middle of those golden streets. So you had just better start learning a few steps yourself, or you're not going to make it. And if that's what church is all about, then I've been misguided all of these years. I'm going to walk out of this church and I will never set foot in another church as long as I live."

About six months later, it was a cold, cold, cold winter. Everything was frozen, solid ice -- and that church caught fire in the night and burned to the ground. Now my father had remarked that night "Something's going to happen; God is gonna strike this church." Fortunately, he always said, he was out on the railroad working.

And that's exactly what happened. We kept on dancing... Lord a' mercy.

CUZ

MATTIE BRANCH

> "There's a land beyond the river
> that they call the Sweet Forever,
> And we only reach that land
> by faith's decree,
> One by one we'll join the portals,
> there to dwell with the immortals,
> When they ring those golden bells
> for you and me..."

I came into this world a menopause mistake... been makin' 'em ever since. My mother died when I was 13 years old. I was nine when she got sick. All the other children were grown except me. In those four years I was very close to her because I was home. I realize now and as I grew older that she knew she was going to die and leave me and she was trying to prepare me, God rest her soul... a lot of it I did not heed to, but some of it comes back and has given me strength that I've needed so many times.

Mother was barely five feet tall, with steel sky-blue eyes. She could just cut her eyes around and look at you and you'd burrow your own hole in the ground... she could put that triple-whammy on you. She was a volume of encyclopedias within herself... this lady was philosophical, smart, a fine Christian lady, and soft-spoken (not a loud-mouth, like my daddy, screamin' and hollerin' and dancin'). My sister Agnes, who became my closest friend, had Mother's personality... the softness. As does my daughter Pat.

cuz

I would wake up on a summer morning and hear Mother out in the flower garden -- the sun never touched her skin... She'd have on a big straw hat with her smock and gloves, stockin's and shoes... and she'd be talking to the flowers. "Oh, you're so beautiful... God made you so beautiful... what a wonderful world this is..." She would sing and hum... "Heavenly sunlight, heavenly sunlight, spreading my soul with glory divine..." Her favorite hymn, which was sung at her funeral, was "When They Ring Those Golden Bells."

Many times Mother would be lying in bed and she'd say, "Doris, will you go in there and play the piano and sing my song for me?" And when she was feelin' a little bit better, she'd say, "Will you get your dancin' board and put it there in front of the door and do a little show for me?" I loved that, too. I'd put on my tappin' shoes, get my dancin' board, and sing and tap dance for her.

WTJS radio had a show every Saturday morning — the "Orange Crush Kiddie Club." Jimmy Allen played the piano while I'd sing and dance. So I got to entertain all the civic clubs with songs like "Eastbound Train," a popular Depression tune. The Exchange Club asked me to sing and dance at their national convention in Memphis at the Peabody Hotel. Well, of course, I was thrilled to death. Daddy said I could go because George and Elizabeth Smith were going to take me over there. I was really dressed-up... a short lavender organdy dress with puffed sleeves; it had one ruffle right up under another and lavender tights underneath; white shoes, white socks; lavender ribbon in my hair.

The Peabody had two roofs, an enclosed roof and this open roof. They had the banquet on the open roof. I sang "Organ Grinder Swing" and "Dark Town Strutter's Ball." And I'll never forget, the national president's wife laid a ten-dollar bill in my hand and I had never seen a ten-dollar bill before. I almost danced off the roof of the Peabody. I thought, I are a star. After the banquet, they carried me over to the other roof and this orchestra, Harry Owen and his Royal Hawaiians, were playing over there. Every night WMC would broadcast the orchestra -- "Way Down South In Dixie."

Mother was listening to the orchestra. She listened every night. When they brought me home, which was way in the night, she said "Oh my dear, I was listening to the orchestra and they said 'And here is little Doris Branch from Jackson, Tennessee, with special entertainment for the National Exchange Convention.' And I was so proud, you are really my star."

Mother always said, "Now, Doris, all ladies learn how to sew and embroider and do handwork. That's what ladies do in the afternoon. You do your work in the morning and you watch and you learn how to cook."

I had my own embroidery hoops. That meant absolutely nothing to me. I needed that like I needed another hole through my head. She got a little tea towel... and every afternoon I would get started in a little wicker rocking chair...

I'd sit down and have my embroidery thread and needle and hoops and she'd give me the towel, saying, "Now this is cross-stitching."

Well, that was pure, hard labor for me. When she would be out of sight, in the house doing something else, I'd lay the stuff down and go out on the stepping stones, singing and tap dancing and doing a show -- play like I had a big audience there.

One day she was standing in the door and caught me. I looked around at her and she said, "You just don't like to do embroidery or handwork, do you?"

"No, ma'am."

"Well, you know, all ladies do that."

"Yes, ma'am." 'Cause I never talked back to her in my life. She didn't allow it.

With a gleam in her eye, she looked at me and said, "Well, you won't be like other ladies, but you're going to have a lot of fun."

How right she was.

We were sitting on the back porch one hot afternoon drinking lemonade. Looking out through the palings of the fence I could see this old hen... peckin' away in the dirt, after a kernel of corn. I watched it and, finally, the old hen picked up the corn.

"Mother, look at that old hen out there. She pecked in that dirt and pecked in that dirt and then, finally, she picked up the kernel of corn."

"Doris, you won't understand this now, but someday you will. That's like life. Sometimes you have to eat a lot of dirt before you get to the corn. And sometimes the more dirt you eat, the sweeter the corn when you get to it." She was some kind a' lady.

Living there on the highway, I think the house was marked... these hobos would knock on our back door... I mean, they looked like they would slit your throat for a dollar and then charge you fifty cents for bleeding. They'd give Mother some sad story... and it'd be cold... She would fix 'em food and give 'em a little lunch to take with 'em. If they were able-bodied folks, she'd ask them to bring a load of wood or coal in, give 'em a coal scuttle and they'd go out and get some coal and put it on the porch for her.

My mother never turned away a soul in her life who needed something to eat. She always shared everything she had.

Daddy used to come home and say "I'm going to find you and my baby here bludgeoned to death. Somebody is gonna come and just knock you in the head."

Mother said "Well, they'll just have to knock me in the head because I cannot turn anybody away who's hungry."

When Daddy was out on the railroad, Mother let me sleep with her. We were in the back bedroom on the north; one of the windows was right there on the back porch. Of course there was no such thing as air-conditioning. It was a hot summer night. My brother John Lee and his wife Ruby were living with us and they were up in the front bedroom.

I had rolled over in the corner and Mother had put her pillow in the window which was even with the bed. She was lying there and felt a nudge, looked up, and through the screen she saw two men. They were cutting the screen. And she smelled something funny... it was chloroform.

She eased out on her stomach, got in the middle of the floor and screamed. The men just kept cuttin' the screen on the window. Mother ran up the hall to the phone by the front door. I ran and got right by her as she was trying to call the police.

In the meantime, John Lee hollered "I'll get 'em!" He ran down the hall from the living room; he had to open a door to get into the back hall. In the corner, by the back door in the hall, we had a rifle. Also somebody had put the broom there in the same corner. These men were still cuttin' the screen. John Lee

CUZ

grabbed for the rifle and knocked over this big heavy broom. That broom handle hit the linoleum floor and it sounded like a gun goin' off, in the middle of the night.

The burglars thought he had shot at them. And he thought they had shot at him. They jumped the bannister on the back porch and went flyin' off.

John Lee came staggering up the hall, shoutin' "Oh, Mama, Mama, they hit me! Oh, they got me, Mama, they got me!"

Daddy railroaded in his sleep. He'd say "Coupla cars, coupla cars..." One night, in the summertime, he had hung his pants on the corner of the bed. Mother heard somebody come down the hall. Whoever this was turned into the bedroom, tiptoed up and lifted Daddy's pants off the bedpost and went up the hall.

Mother tried to wake Daddy up. The burglar had walked right in the house, took Daddy's billfold and, of course, that had his annual pass in it. An annual pass is like a credit card for a railroad man, you can ride anywhere you want with it. The whole family could ride for free. Finally, Daddy jumped up in his BVDs that came just above his knees. He reached over and grabbed the poker that Mother had used to clean the fireplace.

And here he went, flyin' out the door, down the Nashville highway chasin' that burglar in his little BVDs. Called him every kind of son-of-a-bitch in the world... and we were standin' on the corner watchin' him. Mother got tickled. The cars speedin' up and down the highway and Daddy runnin', hollerin', wavin' that poker in the air. Realizing the futility of all this, he came back, steppin' on rocks, trying to stay on the asphalt... screaming at the top of his lungs.

On my 13th birthday Mother wanted to have my picture made and took me down to the New Southern Hotel where Olan Mills had set up shop for photography.

I said "What I want most for my birthday, Mother, is a picture of you."

"Okay, we'll have one made together and I'll get one of you by yourself."

I didn't realize what the next few months would bring...

I was invited by Noel Sherrod, my first love, to go to the SPO fraternity formal dance. Mother said I could go.

"You go down to Nathan's and tell Mr. Nathan that you need a formal dress."

It was my first formal and I was so excited. But Nathan's clothes were not cheap, and I decided I was gonna save some money so Mother would be proud of me. I went to see Grace Hastings and Virgie Duncan, who used to sew for us. They helped me get the material and Virgie was gonna make my dress.

That morning before I left to catch a streetcar to go to town, I went into Mother's bedroom to kiss her goodbye...

She took my hand and said, in a very soft tone, "Doris, you have been a joy to me. I want you to always keep that bubbling personality and that big smile. You're smart and you're talented, and God has a reason for you to be on this earth. Promise me that you'll work hard and that you'll graduate from high school. I want you to know that you've been the light of my life."

"Thank you, Mother. Yes, I promise."

And I went trippin' out. I didn't know that she was telling me goodbye.

cuz

Her funeral was held at Brown's Church, where Mother and Daddy are buried, along with two of my sisters, Martha Louise, who died right after she was born, and Dorothy B., who was barely three years old. John Lee was the oldest child; then Agnes Maureen; then Jenny Mae; then me. This was the only other time that Daddy set foot in a church, since he was "ousted" for dancing years before.

Ewing Griffin, Sr. and Mother were lifelong friends... he was out in front of the house on the highway stopping traffic as they took the body out and put it in the hearse. Daddy went out with Jenny, John Lee and Ruby.

Nobody said anything to me, so I just sat down on the doorstep. I looked up and saw the police, my mother's body go by, the pallbearers; and then I saw Agnes, who was pregnant with Sonny, and her husband Aaron B. Robinson... Aaron had a black Ford with yellow spoke wheels... he happened to look back toward the house and saw me sitting on the doorstep. I never had such a feeling in my life as I did sitting there. I felt like I was totally alone -- nobody cared and there I was -- everybody grown but me.

Aaron slammed on his brakes, sat down on his horn, and everybody turned around like, what in the world?! He got out and said, "Ewing, stop this whole procession! Stop it! We're leaving the one that she loved the most."

He came over to the steps, picked me up bodily, took me to the car and slipped me in between him and Agnes. He said, "Everybody hold it just a minute"... looked at me and said, "Let me tell you somethin', honey. As long as I am living, you don't have to worry about anything. You understand that? Whatever problem you have, you come to me."

And he stuck his head out the window and stated, "We can go on now with the procession."

By the cemetery, in Brown's Methodist Church, I sat between Agnes and Aaron... little country church, neat as a pin... sweet. Brother Skinner got up to preach the funeral...

He said "Well, I look down and see that baby girl there, Doris. I'll always remember one Sunday I was preaching, and Mrs. Branch was seated in the congregation with Doris. I found out later Doris wanted to come down and sit on the front seat where some of the children sat, and Mrs. Branch wouldn't let her..."

... I was thinking, Lord knows, she wouldn't let me. She held onto my coattail, if I got to wigglin' too much -- I think that's why my arms from above my elbows never did get very big, because that's where she'd grab ahold and squeeze and then my whole arm would go numb. And for the rest of church I'd sit there and look at it because she told me, if I didn't sit still (I never could sit still in my life), that one day she'd grab ahold and the arm would fall off. Oh, I believed her...

The congregation got up to sing a song, and then Mother sat down and turned loose of my coattail long enough to straighten her dress. When she did, I went flyin' down the aisle... I don't remember this; but they said I wasn't over three years old. Instead of sitting down there on the seat, I went and sat on the top step to the pulpit and looked up at Brother Skinner. All the kids started gigglin' and I just stood up and said 'Y'all hush and let Brother 'Kinner preach!'

He related this during Mother's funeral... "And she sat back down and looked up at me. I was worried that Sunday about my sermon, but I changed it when I looked down into those little bright blue eyes staring at me in adoration. I preached on 'Suffer the little children to come unto Me, for theirs is the Kingdom of Heaven.' That was one of my best sermons -- I feel like God sent that little girl right down that aisle. After church services, I said 'Y'all leave my baby alone... Mrs. Branch, I don't wanna catch you doing anything to her.' I wish everybody would come and get that close to the pulpit... then we wouldn't have near the problems we have today."

After Mother died, it was tough. But that's why I've always had such a hangup... I prayed so hard, guess I aggravated God... sometimes I felt like He unplugged me... that I would live to see all my children grown.

WAR OF THE WORLDS

I'm 13 years old and I'm thinking, holy mackerel! It was Sunday night, I was sitting in Calvary Baptist church, and the preacher was well into his sermon.

Here comes this man cavortin' down the aisle. He and the preacher start whisperin' back and forth, back and forth...

All of a sudden, the minister, Brother Black, held up his hand and said "Oh, brethren, we've got to get closer to God, closer to God! I'm tellin' you, there's a terrible thing that's happenin'... these 20-foot men from Mars are invading Earth. I understand that they are now in North Carolina and they're headed this way! So we're gonna have a prayer here... they're taking the country! I want everybody to go home so we can all be with our families when it happens!"

Well, it scared the pea-eye goose water out of me. I was thinking... Oh Lord, I'm sorry I did that... I'm sorry... People got on their knees... some of these women talking about the affairs they had had because their backs were up against the wall, they were fixin' to get stomped by men 20 feet tall from Mars. It was unreal!

I left church, ran home, kept looking behind me, just knowing that one of those big men was gonna come and step on me and mash me flat into nothing.

Some little old ladies were practically having heart attacks... said they were seein' 'em coming across the orchard.

No one seemed to know it was that Orson Welles radio show.

DIXIE AROMA

Fulton, Kentucky was to be my new home at the age of 14 when my father remarried. My first stepmother made life very hard for me, but when I walked into Fulton High School the first person I saw was this girl. She said "You're the new girl in town, aren't you?"

"Yes. My name's Doris Branch."

"My name is Maureen Ketchum and I'm your friend." She's been my friend ever since.

The kids at school were fabulous to me, and they helped make my life a little easier.

The night I graduated from high school, Agnes tried to get to Fulton but had a tire blow-out. This was during the war and we had ration coupons; you couldn't get tires. My father was at home and my stepmother told him that he needed to rest. She went, but she wasn't my family. I graduated third highest in my class, and not a soul of my family was there. As my mother used to say, you try to make things make you better instead of bitter.

I received some honors and felt like Mother was there in spirit, as I was keeping my promise. (All other education had to be self-inflicted.)

There was an annual Strawberry Festival in Paducah, Kentucky... Dixie Aroma Strawberries, including a beauty pageant where the girls wore evening gowns. I was voted Western Kentucky Strawberry Queen... Dixie Aroma (call me "Stinky" for short) and Miss Fulton County. My stepmother made me leave the Queen's Ball, but it's a fond memory up till that point...

I guess they felt sorry for me 'cause they never had another Strawberry Festival after that. I suppose I spoiled the crop.

cuz

GETTING OUT

When the Japanese bombed Pearl Harbor, I was riding around in a car with a bunch of girls. I had started dating James Herman Freeman... he was eight years older than me and I thought that was hot stuff. He was good-lookin', wore gray slacks and white sweaters and drove a spotless, pretty car. I was infatuated.

He joined the Navy and I was there, with his foster mother, when he was sworn in. She was a very fine lady... dignified... the Old South. She put the engagement ring on my finger 'cause Jimmy was in the service. So that summer I was very close to his mother and that September I was enrolling in Murray State Teachers College. They called me one night and said Mrs. Freeman had had a heart attack and wanted to see me, so I rushed down there. When I walked in the front door she breathed her last breath. I never did know what she wanted to tell me.

James Herman flew to Memphis and was home two weeks for the funeral. He wanted me to come to California, so I did. My father got me a railroad pass. Went to college three days altogether... I matriculated, then I exited.

We married in November of '42... beautiful wedding. The church was full of people that I'd never seen before. The town, Oceanside, gave us the wedding, planned as a surprise by Bill and Lottie Moore. We called them Uncle Bill and Aunt Lottie. Jimmy had met them at the USO. They took us in and we became fast friends... called me Sugarfoot. When Pat was a baby, they drove all the way from California to Tennessee to see us.

Big headlines in the paper: STRAWBERRY QUEEN MARRIES SAILOR.

The day I married I kissed 120 men, countin' him. The whole company stood in line and every one of 'em kissed me. At the ripe old age of seventeen. I lied about my age on the marriage certificate. Aunt Lottie and Uncle Bill had this great big Buick and all their friends pitched in their rationed gas coupons and they took us to Del Rio By The Sea for our honeymoon.

We were married a little over two months when he left for the South Pacific. I already had my ticket to go back home, and Aunt Lottie went to Los Angeles with me to the train station.

Before boarding the train, I purchased some Tampax, as I was having my period... I thought that would be big-time, since I was married... like that has anything to do with it. I inserted the thing and it was uncomfortable. On the train, I had to sit sideways... all the way from Los Angeles to St. Louis, where I had to change trains. Finally, I realized that there's a little round cardboard thing they put around 'em that's the cover... but country here didn't remove it. I inserted the whole cotton-pickin' thing, so it's a wonder I hadn't injured myself good fashion. Evidently I didn't because I gave birth to four children after that. It taught me a lesson — read the instructions. We don't go by the directions too well in our family.

The marriage itself was not to last, as eventually Jimmy and I grew apart. But we sure could have babies!...

BIRTH CONTROL AND ALL MY CHILDREN

Two little boys in kindergarten were talkin'... one said "Hey, I found a condom on our veranda!" Other little boy said "What's a veranda?"

Birth control never worked for me. My first-born, Pat, was rhythm... somehow I got off-beat; my second-born, Cindie, was diaphragm... my third-born, Jim, was condom... and my fourth-born, Connie, was vasectomy... God, I kept lookin' for those three fellas ridin' those camels, be stompin' through my back yard lookin' for a star; like I don't care what star you're followin', but get them camels outta my garden, you're messin' up my spring onions, baby.

When Pat was two years old in nursery school, they had the Christmas play... the Nativity scene with a play-like baby Jesus... and then they started singing. Pat was all gussied-up in a little red-plaid dress. She was sittin' there pattin' her foot where the younger children were gathered. They were singin' "Silent Night."

When they finished, all of a sudden, Pat started singin' "Bongo bongo bongo, I don't wanna leave the Congo, oh no no no no no -- Benga banga bongo, I'm so happy in the Congo, I refuse to go!" That was a song that was real popular at the time.

I immediately had to get her by the hand and out of there and tell her, you don't sing things like that... but everybody got a big kick out of it. They said, "Well, look whose child she is..."

In the church nursery one day -- Pat was four years old -- they said "Anybody wanna sing a song?"

Pat said "I do."

She got up and sang "I'm my own grandma, it's the derndest mixup"... all the way through. The lyrics aren't the easiest in the world to learn either. So Pat has entertained in her life a good bit, too...

When Cindie was born, Pat was 16 months old. Cindie looked so much like my sister Jenny, a little Kewpie doll. She started having ear infections at seven months and then what we were told was strep throat. I was rocking and holding her when she bowed her back and went into a convulsion, started having a seizure, and scared the putty out of me. I thought if I could get her to Dr. Swan Burrus, everything would be all right. I called Agnes and asked her to meet me at Fitts-White Clinic.

When I walked in the door, I just pitched Cindie into Dr. Burrus' arms and we went flyin' upstairs. He started working with her, and then here came Agnes and Aaron and the whole entourage. We really looked terrible. Jimmy was working at the Post Office, so they went and got him.

Dr. Burrus said "Agnes, get Doris out of here. There's no point in her seeing this."

Miss Lovey Reed, who was the Head Nurse at the clinic, ran down the hall with oxygen, and I knew somethin' was wrong. They opened that door and Dr. Burrus had Cindie by the heels; she was limp and turning dark.

He said "It's too late, this baby's dead."

I fell apart. But she responded to the oxygen and went into a coma. They isolated her because they didn't know what the problem was. I was smoking at that time and Cindie would get into my cigarettes, cut those eyes around at me with that little impish grin and go "errrrrrr," take each cigarette, tear it, sprinkle the tobacco... pinch 'em and tear 'em up. Agnes brought me a carton of cigarettes, although I couldn't smoke in the room.

They gave Cindie ether and, during the night, her muscles began to get rigid. I hollered and the nurses gave her a shot to relax the muscles. I had my head layin' down on the bed and my hand patting Cindie... she opened her eyes and said "Mommy."

I jumped straight up. I opened those cigarettes by the pack and she had tobacco all over that room.

That was her first attack of a kidney disease, pilonephritis, which she had until she was eleven years old. Dr. Oliver Graves worked with her for years, in and out of the hospital, and cured her.

My son, Jim ("Little Jimmy"), used to go see God when he was a little boy. He had his little boxer shorts on and he always wanted to wear a little cap... and he had a broom handle that leaned up against the back of the door...   After he finished his breakfast, he said "Me going to see God, Mommy."

I said "Okay."

Every morning he'd walk up in between the houses and the neighbors would say "Where you goin', Little Jimmy?" "Me goin' to see God."

One morning I followed him. He went up there in the woods, stood there and talked to a bush. I thought, Mmmmm. That could be some heavy stuff, so I left him alone.
Finally, one morning he came in, lip just dragging, all puckered down, pitiful... and I said "Little Jimmy? Did you go see God?"

"Um-hmm, but He wadn't there."

"How did you know He wasn't there?"

"He disciples told me He wadn't there."

And he never did go back to see God. That was really interesting.

When he was little-bitsy, he'd sit down in the floor and listen to classical music by himself, thoroughly enraptured. I guess I think he's sorta special...

Connie, my youngest, had a virus that was going into colitis when she was four months old. Oller (Frances Oller, but we called her 'Oller' -- a wonderful friend and neighbor) came over and said we should give her a tea enema. So we did, and it worked... Oller was the Earth Mother to all babies. She knew what to do.

Connie looked up at Oller and started whistling... she whistled in two notes. Dr. Burrus said he could not believe this baby was whistling without a tooth in her head. The word got out that she whistled; and, being the ham that she was at that age, she loved it. She would sit in her playpen shakin' a rattle and whistling.

And I had to take her to all the pediatricians... Dr. Burrus wanted to show her off because this was The Whistler. She's been puckered up to whistle ever since.

TO DYE FOR

or

"Am I Blue!"

Pat and Cindie were babies when, one day I had a terrible stomachache and it got worse in the night. I went down to Fitts-White Clinic; they took my blood count and it was a little high, but they said give it 24 hours and see. The pain got a little better, but my stomach was so sore.

The next morning I got up about five o'clock... back then the big thing was pastel colored curtains and I had some blue ruffled curtains in my bedroom. I was house-cleaning and this morning I had planned to Rit the curtains — re-dye them — 'cause they had faded in the sun at the windows. I put 'em in the dye and it took a while to process.

In the meantime, Pat and Cindie woke up and I fed them. About ten o'clock they called me from Fitts-White Clinic and said "Doris, you need to come on down here. Dr. Burrus wants to check your white count again to be sure that everything's okay."

"I'm all right, a little sore; but I'm okay."

I was hungry from being up so early, so I fixed myself some creamed dry beef on toast — it makes me shudder to even think about the stuff now — and I didn't even bathe. I just washed my face and away I went to the clinic. Thought I'd be right back — didn't happen.

When I got there, they pricked the finger and I waited.

They said "You've got a hot appendix."

The next thing I knew they were prepping me and rolling me into surgery. I was transferred to the operating table and they slapped ether on my face and I was about to slide under.

All of a sudden, somebody knocked the fool outta me — shook me! — hit me! — slapped me!! I opened my eyes and Dr. White, the surgeon, was leanin' over me with his mask on...

"What in the hell is the matter with your hands and arms?!"

I looked up about half-swacked from ether. "I've been... dyein'... some curtains... blue... this mornin'..."

"My God, I thought you were already dead and rigor mortis had set in! It's a good thing you told me that. I mighta shipped you on to the funeral home."

They finished the surgery and rolled me out.

My ever-abiding sister Agnes didn't get there until after I was in surgery. When they rolled me out, my hands and arms were out over the sheet. I was out like a light. Agnes began to cry...

"Oh my Lord, what's happened to her?"

Dr. White said "Well, God, don't worry about it. She dyed some curtains blue. I thought she'd died, too, and had already turned blue."

Penicillin had just come into being — my fever shot up and they gave me a shot — the needle was so big that a time or three it bounced offa my back-end.

Ether and creamed beef... ad nauseam.

THE BIRTH OF "COUSIN TUNY"

In the early forties, my brother-in-law Aaron started a chain of radio stations in the South -- The Dixie Broadcasting Network. We opened WDXI radio where I did programming and on the air with Miss Billie Walker. I went into Sales in radio, the first woman to sell radio advertising in Jackson. The station ran from 5:00 in the morning until 7:00... you had hillbilly music (they didn't call it country music back then, it was hillbilly music)... from 11:00 to 12:00 you had the Farm and Home Hour. We had a 30-minute live show. From the studios we had a hillbilly band and we sang and gave the commercials. I did five minutes on the air every day, singing with the band -- real country, country.

Aaron said, "Okay, Doris, it's time for you to do some stuff, whatever you want to do."

I was always singing 'I'm a lonely little petunia in an onion patch, an onion patch.' I called Pat, my oldest daughter, 'Petunia' before she was born. And I used to call everybody 'Cousin.'

So I said, "Well, I tell you what. I wanna be Cousin Petunia -- that's gonna be the name."

Agnes interjected, "Now let's think about this a minute. You sing, and you dance, and you play musical instruments."

"Well, yeah, I'm an illegitimate musician... I play in the cracks of the keys." (I'm like the monkey on the pickle barrel playin' a fiddle in the store... when a customer asked the owner if the monkey knew his butt's in the brine, the owner said 'I don't know, but if you'll hum it, he'll try to play it.')

Agnes said, "Why don't you call her Tuny?"

The T-u-n-y is just puny with a T.

The basic idea was to be a countrier-than-country comic.

When I step into my alter ego's pantaloons, I step into another realm... it's the closest thing to looking at the world through rose-colored glasses.

"THE COUSIN TUNY SHOW"

This live TV program was sort of a spin-off from Circle 7 Theater with "Cousin Tuny and her Little Cousins," the first Tuny children's show, originating from WDXI-Television Theater, which accommodated a live audience of 300 people. The first outing was longer and more involved. And we decided to trim down, change around, simplify. Thus, we segued into our Birthday format in the studio.

We had this little chair that was covered in gold -- the child sat there kind of elevated -- and I had two crowns, a boy's crown and a girl's crown.

"The Birthday Cousin wears the crown, the birthday crown." I put the crown on the child's head. They'd move in for a closeup of him/her. The child would invite twelve of his or her friends to be on the show with them, and we'd have a party.

An American flag was on the set, and first thing was to pledge allegiance; a commercial, Dr. Pepper or Coca-Cola or Kas potato chips. Sealtest milk was with me the entire twelve year run.

"It's time for The Cousin Tuny Show, so gather 'round, Little Cousins. Now here she is -- Cousin Tuny!"

"Well, a big old howdy-do, Little Cousins. Gee, you're lookin' great today. We're gonna have a lot of fun. And today we're celebrating a birthday of Mary Sue Smith."

The Cousin Tuny Show Theme was "The Doll Dance" by Russ Morgan's Orchestra. There was a backdrop with "Tuney's Little Cousins" painted on it -- and my character's face in the center. It was erroneously painted 'Tuney' instead of 'Tuny'... but since we were on such a low budget back then, in the 50's, the early days of TV, we left it just like that 'cause we couldn't afford to redo it. (However, as the years have flown by, I've been mispronounced and misspelled in all sorts of ways... Toonie, Tuna... just call me Charlie for short.)

My outfit was a checkered dress, pantaloons to match and high-top shoes. Blacked out my two front teeth and put freckles across my nose. When I went to television, I decided to put on a hat -- I put pipe cleaners in the front with a daisy on the top. And I always said that that was my TV antenna, those pipe cleaners. The real antenna at WDXI at that time covered parts of Mississippi, Kentucky and, of course, Tennessee. Every show was telecast completely live. What an experience!

"Now we wanna talk to some of the Little Cousins."

cuz

I started at the end, squatted down, and talked to them.

"What is your name?"

"Joe Brown."

"How old are you, Joe?"

"I'm five years old."

"That's a whole fistful of fingers, isn't it?"

"Uh-huh."

"Joe, what do you wanna be when you get big?"

"I want to be a fireman."

"Did your momma tell you somethin' you shouldn't do?"

"Told me not to pick my nose."

I heard that a lot o' times. About that time, they'd stick their finger right up their nose just as far as they could get it.

"Who do you wanna say hello to?"

"I wanna say hello to my momma and my daddy and my brother and my sister, my aunt and uncle..."

"Look up there in that little red light and wave to em."

"Now, you wanna perform or you wanna be entertained?" If they said they wanna be entertained, I'd go to the next child. If they wanted to perform, "What do you wanna do? Wanna sing a song or hop on one foot?" They'd take it from there.

On to the next child... "Oh, this is the prettiest dress you have on. Do you have a boyfriend? How old do you think you oughta be before you get married?"

"Eight. Never gonna get married, but I'm gonna have a baby. Wanna be a mother."

"When you get married."

"No, never gonna get married. Just gonna be a mother."

A little Jewish boy, who is now a surgeon out west, was about the fifth child down one day and I asked who he wanted to say hello to.

"My momma, my daddy and my sister and my brother and the Rabbi."

"Oh, I know the Rabbi and he is so fine. Is he watching you?"

"Yes, ma'am, he's watchin'. He watches you every day, Cousin Tuny."

"That's wonderful. Look up there in the red light and wave at 'em."

"You gonna perform or you gonna be entertained?"

"I'm gonna perform."

"What are you gonna do?"

"I'm gonna sing a song."

"You wanna dedicate this to somebody?"

"Uh-huh, I wanna dedicate this to the Rabbi."

"Alright, look right up there in the camera, in that red light. And Rabbi, this is for you."

He stood up and sang, "Jesus loves me, this I know..." all the way through. Which rocked the Jewish Temple for sure.

I interviewed the birthday child, and three or four more children, and we'd show a Cartuny... Looney Tunes and Deputy Dog... When I first went on the air we had Roy Rogers and Gene Autry movies. We'd play part of 'em and come back and

CUZ

interview some of the children and do another Cartuny.

Now it's BIRTHDAY time. The birthday cake was rolled out, the candles lit, and we sang: "Our Cousins have a birthday, we're so glad. And we know how many they have had. As we light the candles we are told, our Cousins are one more year old"...

I read the names of the children sent in through the mail, their birthdays, and we wished them all a happy birthday. The little birthday child made a wish and blew out the candles. Another Cartuny or a commercial, while they moved the table out with the birthday cake, and I finished interviewing the children.

They changed the set to little sawbuck tables for the children to have supper with me. We had hot dogs, Sealtest milk and Sealtest ice cream. We sang the Sealtest song that I wrote the lyrics to:

"I drink Sealtest, yessiree, Sealtest is the milk for me. It'll always taste so good to you, makes you strong and healthy too. Hahaha, you and me, we drink Sealtest, yessiree. Hahaha, you and me, we drink Sealtest -- yessiree bobolinko!" We gave the blessing.

"God is great, God is good, and we thank Him for our food. By His hand we all are fed, He gives to us our daily bread. Amen."

During supper we'd slip in another Cartuny and, carrying on, I read any interesting mail, or if I had a special somebody who was sick in the hospital... if it was on a Thursday, when I would visit the children in the hospital: "I'm on my way out to General Hospital. I've got some toys for everybody, so everybody be sure to take your medicine and do what the nurses tell you to do so you'll get well and be happy and healthy and wonderful.

And to all my Little Cousins: Don't forget to clean your plate and pick up your toys, and don't forget to say your prayers. And don't you never ever forget, you're tops with Tuny because you're all Tuny's Cousins. I love you. Until tomorrow, 'bye-'bye out there." The Theme Song...

Announcer: "Tune in again tomorrow for 'The Cousin Tuny Show.' If you would like to have a birthday party on 'The Cousin Tuny Show,' or if you would like your birthday mentioned, send your name and your address to Cousin Tuny, WDXI-TV, Jackson, Tennessee."

... One time the show was over -- they gave me two minutes and I said, "We have two minutes and we've done everything we were gonna do. Anybody wanna do anything?"

CUZ

This little towheaded boy sittin' there at the sawbuck table said "I'll say a poem." He was five years old. (Nothin' like a five-year-old.) He stood up and looked into the camera and said, like he was reciting the 23rd Psalm: "Birdie, birdie, in the sky, that did dukey in my eye, I don't worry, I don't cry, I'm just proud that cows don't fly." And he sat down. We flat went to automation.

... We had a little boy who had his hand in his britches playin' with himself. He got up to sing, and the rhythm of the hand and the way he sang were in sync. He started out singin': "Oh well, he sings, swing your music to the cattle as he swings, back-and-forth-in-the-saddle -on-his-horse, pretty-good-horse" -- the little britches were just a-movin' -- he had that hand down there really goin' to town. I could hear 'em screamin' "Get a closeup of his face!" They had a full shot of him and you could see what he was doin.'

... A little boy said to me, "Cousin Tuny, my momma is so unhappy."

"Oh, well, you must start pickin' up your toys and clean your plate and tell her how much you love her."

"Not my fault. It's Daddy's."

"Oh."

"I got a big secret to tell you if you won't tell anybody."

"I won't tell a soul." And there I was with that hot mike in my hand.

"Momma cries every night."

"I'm so sorry. You have to try to make her happy."

"I can't. It's Daddy's fault. She's gonna have a baby, but she don't want anybody to know it. She says she's too old.

She don't need any more babies."

"Well, I won't tell a soul." That woman -- I thought she was gonna kill him when it was over.

There were the times that I'd have a child on the show who was terminally ill.

A little girl from Paris, Tennessee was in the hospital. And she wanted to be on my show so bad. They gave her a pass out of the hospital and brought her down to appear. I went to see her before she died, soon after that. Those are the things I shall never forget.

Once I was talkin' to a little girl... "Who do you wanna say hello to?"

"Momma and Daddy, my neighbors and my grandmother -- and Mrs. Buck."

And the little girl sittin' next to her said, "Mrs. Buck died last week. She's not watchin'."

"Why, she certainly is. Don't you know that they watch Cousin Tuny in heaven? They have television up there."

Out of the mouths of babes...

THE DIXIE REBEL BAND

The Elks Club, in a great big ol' house that was converted into a private club, was up on College Street. Daddy loved to rare back at the bar with that cigar in his mouth and drink beer and tell jokes. Miss Evie (my #2 stepmother) and I would play slot machines while people danced. Jamie O'Neill led a Big Band that I sang with, and Jimmy Allen took over the band when Jamie got sick.

Kemmons Wilson built his second Holiday Inn out on 45 North, where I played marimba and sang with Charlie Baker's Dance Band on Saturday nights... Now Miss Billie Walker -- she was a long tall drink o' water; her hair was bleached almost white; real country -- had a hillbilly band that I sang with. That was back in the days that hillbilly bands didn't amplify any of the instruments. You just stood up there with a microphone.

Jerry Geter... a great big old fat boy... played mandolin, slapped a bass fiddle fantastic, and had a great singin' voice. Some of the other hillbillies came in and out like a revolving door.

The Dixie Rebels -- my first band -- became the second Cousin Tuny Show on TV. In the Dixie Rebel Band, we didn't do just country. My daughter Cindie appeared weekly and became "Little Tuny." She was about nine years old and was dressed identically to me. She sang hymns and songs of the era, like "Rockin' Around The Clock." Ione Tillman (we called her "Ludy") played the rinky-tink piano -- Howard Glisson ("Slick") played drums and was famous for singin' "Your Cheatin' Heart" -- Alton Rinks, real tall, black-haired, played lead guitar, worked for the railroad on the side -- Billy DePriest, a redheaded guy, real quiet, laid-back, picked a mean five-string country banjo -- Marvin Adcock, a little round, fat fella, played rhythm guitar. And "Lukey" (his real name was Johnny Glisson, Slick's younger brother) played a bass fiddle. Lukey had false teeth at a very young age, and he was really young then... he'd take out his teeth and put those great big ol' overalls on and we would jitterbug... everybody wanted us to dance. I always did a skit with Lukey and we sang together. Flatt n' Scruggs followed us on Channel 7 live -- they came in and set up their band and we pulled ours out in a hurry.

The Dixie Rebels made all the country schoolhouses in West Tennessee. We'd advertise on the TV program to come out and do shows on percentage, to raise money for different organizations... Little did I realize how this sounded, especially when I announced it on television, but the first two appearances we were called to do were in Sweet Lips one week and Peter's Landing the next. Needless to say, Ludy fell off the piano stool laughing, as did ol' Slick Glisson.

When we went down to Sweet Lips, we had to go across this bridge and underneath the bridge was a big creek with lily pads floatin' around in it -- it was still daylight. Pulled up to this schoolhouse and not a soul anywhere. Well, I got out and rang the bell and here they came.

On the schoolhouse stage was a curtain that was painted like Joe's Store and Drink Coca-Cola and rolled down from the top. It was sort of a canvas thing that had one o' those big hollow aluminum pipes to hold it down. The school was one great big room that had these sliding things, very antique, that came across to separate the rooms. In my dressing room at the side of the stage there was a cord of stove wood.

'Course we had a million dollars' worth of fun... We went there on percentage, 60/40; so when we left, I took the money and divided it evenly among us -- we made six dollars apiece. That was our 60 percent.

When we came back over the bridge, we were all laughing. Ludy had the most infectious laugh I have ever heard. She was sitting in the back seat of the car and she said "Lord God, if some man got me on this bridge over these lily pads and said, either get out or put out, I'd put out 'cause I sure as hell wouldn't walk across these lily pads." We started calling her "Lily Pad" after that, kiddin' her on television... oh boy, those were the days...

TED MACK & THE WASP ATTACK

I used to do a comedy standup act. I sang Dorothy Shay songs... the Park Avenue Hillbilly... and told jokes in between. The Memphis Shrine came over as guests of the Jackson Shrine... they had the Gold Room of the New Southern Hotel and it spilled out into the mezzanine, a ton of people. They introduced me, and Ludy was playing for me. I told a joke or two and sang "Uncle Fud."

Well, I was born in Tennessee

And I was married when I was three

My husband couldn't wait fer me

'Cause he was forty-seven

My kinfolks up and had him hung,

Said I was married much too young

And I must wait 'til I become

A growed-up gal of seven.

So I ups and marries my brother-in-law,

I didn't have to ask my pa

My ma said "Shucks, he ain't yore pa,

Yore pa's yer Uncle Fud"

CUZ

My Uncle Fud said Naw, he warn't...
My Cousin Luke was the guilty varmint
They waylaid Ma that night, consarn it,
Got relatives in my blood.

So that makes my cousin my sister Sue,
Darned if I know who is who
And my nephew is my uncle too,
Just one big happy family.

Well, I gits tired of my brother-in-law
And thought that I would tarry
With my nitwit uncle on my nephew's side,
My nitwit Uncle Harry.

Well, he sits around and he whittles wood,
He goes "Blum, Blum, Blum" and he does it good...
Now I'd shore marry him if I could
But he's got six wives already...

I always wondered what Uncle Harry's got
That makes them women hang around a lot

He chased me once and I got caught...

Way down in Tennessee...

So that's just the reason I long to be

In the hills of Tennessee...

With my Uncle Harry just amusin' me

With his "Blum, Blum, Blum, Blum, Blum"!

I noticed that the Memphis crowd were just courteous in their applause and laughter. I could feel I didn't have them with me all the way. I had Jackson, but not Memphis. I also noticed that there was a white-haired man sittin' there that the Memphis crowd kept lookin' at. He would look up at me, kind of stoical, and then he would look down at the table at his plate.

I told a joke about my cousin bein' a buyer... "My cousin went to New York to buy for the store he worked for, and at the end of the first week he wired his wife and he said 'I can't come home, I'm still buyin'.' At the end of the second week, he wired his wife again and he said 'I can't come home, I'm still buyin'.' At the end of the third week, his wife wired him and said 'If you don't hurry home, I'm gonna start sellin' what you've been buyin'.'"

This little white-haired man roared — he just bent double. And Memphis went wild then. I realized that they were watching his reaction to me. Then I took the ball and ran with it. They gave me a standing ovation and called me back for an encore; and then I wouldn't do any more. It's always best not to give 'em too much sugar for a dime.

cuz

He came up to me and introduced himself as Benny Bluestein. He was a theatrical agent in Memphis. Gave me his card and said "Girl, you need to be out of this town."

"No, I don't. I'm where I need to be."

"Well, I'd like to talk to you... when you're over in Memphis, call me."

I did call him one day and he got me an audition for Ted Mack. I went over to the audition with Ludy and I called Benny Bluestein. He took us to the Variety Club in downtown Memphis, a private theatrical club in the old Claridge Hotel. Benny was very encouraging about expanding and nurturing my career, but I knew that that couldn't happen. It was not my priority at that time. But I would have loved to appear on the Ted Mack Show.

I was called back for the final audition. You were supposed to have music... Ludy had some music, but it was the oboe section for the hen-cackling of some kind of opera or something, I don't know what it was. She put that thing up on the piano — upside down — sat down and commenced to play "Put Your Shoes On, Lucy" just like she was playin' from the music.

> Put your shoes on, Lucy
> Don't you know you're in the city
> Put your shoes on, Lucy
> It's really such a pity
> That Lucy can't go barefoot wherever she goes

> 'Cause she loves to feel
> the wiggle of her toes

Put your shoes on, Lucy
'Cause you're here in old New York
You'll get by alrighty
If you'll let 'em hear you talk
All the city slickers love that
Southern drawl
So give 'em they "honeychile" and "hi, y'all"

Lucy, let the good things happen
Lucy, won't you stop that yappin'
How you act will be the death of me
Don't they got skycrapuhs down in
Tennessee

Put your shoes on, Lucy
Even tho' they kinda pinch
Stop that balkin', you gotta do some walkin'
That's a cinch
Use your party manners, you'll need 'em and how
Put your shoes on, Lucy
You're a big girl now!

    I was informed later that I did not win the appearance on the TV show, it was on national network, because they were told I was professional. Benny Bluestein's interest was flattering, but I always knew I was meant to be where I am today. We had to hustle back to Jackson because Agnes and Aaron were taking me to a show in Dyersburg early the next morning, a Sunday.

Aaron was driving, with Agnes and myself in the front seat. A wonderful black lady, part Indian, Cora, was in the back seat. Cora was born on my grandmother's farm and worked for the family throughout her lifetime. I loved her. We all did. Next to Cora were my niece and nephew, Carol and Sonny.

This was before air-conditioning in automobiles, so the windows were down. We stopped. This church was just lettin' out and there was a house right next door. This lady was sitting on the front porch.

A wasp flew in the window and up my dress — Folks, I came outta that car and I went flyin' up those steps — and I was takin' off clothes big-time-fast!

Aaron was hollerin' "My God, what's the matter with that woman?! Lord, Agnes, do somethin' about her! Go get her!"

I ran in that woman's house, jumpin' up and down like a pogo stick. Of course the wasp flew away — but I almost did too.

Aaron got to laughin'. He said "You did the fastest strip I've ever seen!"

All those people comin' outta church didn't know what to think, not to mention the lady on the porch. She never did leave her chair.

THE MOONGLOWS

For some 25 years the Moonglows Combo consisted of Jerry Van Cleave and Ray Allison and myself. Jerry played a big Hammond organ with Leslie tone cabinets and a moog that was like a sideman -- you could change it and make it sound like a whole orchestra. Ray played drums and sang. And I played marimba, the clavietta (you blow in -- has keys on it, like a piano), shook a tambourine and sang -- you know, you do a little bit of everything when there's just three of you. And my yougest daughter Connie sang with us occasionally.

Our reference to "woodshed" simply meant we'd rehearse, usually in Jerry's apartment. We played country clubs every Saturday night. Most of 'em I enjoyed, but there were some when I was very tired. But now and then they'd start throwing money after four hours on the bandstand; your adrenalin starts shootin' out of every hole you got; and somehow or other...

cuz

The first date we played was a supper club in Donnertown, which wasn't easy to get to... All of Jackson upper-class went up there. This was back in the days when it was dry. I mean dry, dry, dry. This place was a big ol' concrete block building; it wasn't very pretentious looking outside. But when you went in, there was a great big bar and long tables with red and white checkered cloths on them, dance floor, and then the bandstand.

It had been rumored that the Donner family had gotten into trouble. They were watched because people thought they were bootleggin'.

I was on the bandstand and the place was full of people. They had their whiskey bottles on the tables. I had just started singin' "Bill Bailey, Won't You Please Come Home?" And about that time, here came two huge dudes -- Tennessee Highway Patrolmen -- I mean big, tall drinks o' water. They leaned up against the bar and looked at me. I thought, Oh God -- I was doin' the children's TV show during this time -- that's all I need now, just get myself screwed-up in the big time here. I could just see the front page of The Jackson Sun.

So I looked up at 'em and at everybody -- all the whiskey bottles immediately went under the tables. The rumor was that they came by for a payoff. I don't know whether that was true or not. Anyway, I started singin' "Won't you go home, Bill Bailey -- Get yo'self on home!" The Patrolmen started laughin' and left after a little while.

We were playing the Country Club in Savannah, Tennessee on New Year's Eve. We played about six hours and, boy, our butts were draggin'... cold, God, it was so cold... It was about three o'clock in the mornin', came up over the bridge comin' from Savannah after we'd loaded up all the instruments. And, all of a sudden, we heard something go PSSSSSSSSH...

Ray turned around, leaned over me, and said, "Jerry, I

believe we got a flat tire."

Jerry said, "Oh, merciful saints, merciful Father!"

We got over the bridge, pulled off to the side, opened the door and, my God, that wind comin' up off the Tennessee River will cut you a new one. Well, all the flashlights were out. I happened to have a little bitty flashlight on the end of a key chain. I stood out there shakin' and holdin' that little bitty beam flashlight.

Ray yelled, "Oh my God, I feel like I'm fifteen miles from water and covered with shit."

We all fell out laughin' and that sorta loosened things up. That's a good way to express a feeling, when you think you're up that creek without a paddle and no boat.

"MISS HATCHIE BOTTOM"

Bert Parks said "I swear, Tuny, you're the sexiest thing on the boardwalk."

I said "Honey, the sexiest splinter on the boardwalk, that's me... my figure's a perfect 38: 12-14-12. I'm the First Runner-Up to Miss Tennessee."

I wore a 'mock' old-fashioned swimsuit (a la 1907) with my Miss Tennessee rosette, "Miss Hatchie Bottom" banner across me; red, white and blue high-top shoes, striped socks, and pantaloons. In the Miss America Parade, I prissed out there on that boardwalk, went down the middle of a hundred thousand people lined up on either side... and the Tennessee entourage behind me.

For years I was Press Relations and Publicity Manager for the Miss Tennessee Pageant. I sold it, wrote the commercials and put it together... then we -- WDXI radio, my dear friend Ruth O'Neill Anderson, who was Aaron's right hand at the station and has been close to me through it all -- covered the broadcast for ten years at the Miss America Pageant in Atlantic City. We always had seats in front of Convention Hall for the parade.

During the parade, when I was decked-out as 'Miss Hatchie Bottom,' I looked up and, comin' down the boardwalk, steppin' high, was the Mummers' Band. The leader, with all the fancy plumes and spangles and everything, was doin' the cakewalk.

I said, "Well, I can't stand this. I'll see y'all later."

I got out there, grabbed him by the arm, and here I go, leading the Mummers' Band. He said "Who in the hell are you?"

"I'm Miss Tennessee's First Runner-Up, and she ain't near as sexy as I am."

I just could not sit still with all those banjos playin' and all those gorgeous plumes and beautiful costumes. We had a big time.

Ironically, several years later, I was in Philadelphia at the National Meeting of the American Women in Radio and Television. Marlo Thomas was speaking at the banquet, with about 750 people. I had on a white tuxedo with a black stripe down the side and black lapels... I'm sitting there and they open up the doors and here comes the Mummers' Band. Well, I was screwin' a hole in the seat. I looked around for my friend, the leader. The band played two or three numbers, and then they started doin'... "Ya da da da da da da da da da da da" ("Dixie")... and here he came through the door with all those big plumes behind him.

I went "Yeee-hooo" -- gave a big Rebel Yell -- and I went over there and grabbed him by the arm. I said "You remember me? Only I had on my sexy swimsuit... you and I went down the boardwalk."

"Oh my God, I wondered what happened to you!"
"Here I am... just look a little different than I did last time."

"Yes, you do, but I remember you... how could I not?"

At the Miss America Pageant, they always had a party on Thursday night for the former Miss Americas and all the high moguls. They made a big presentation to me about the third or fourth year I was there -- gave me a T-shirt -- on the front are two fried eggs and underneath it says, in great big letters: IN CASE OF RAPE, THIS SIDE UP.

I said "My mother thanks you, my father thanks you... I want to thank my writers, my director..."

On Friday night the Pageant had a big party for all the Southern states... an orchestra and all that jazz... big thing. When I got to the Howard Johnson, where we were staying, I told my cohorts I had to go up and leave my tape recorder, etc., and I'd be back down. I had on a tuxedo. Left my tuxedo pants on and put that T-shirt on.

Went back downstairs and called the bellhop, gave him a tip and I said "I want you to go in there, stop the orchestra, tell the orchestra leader I want him to roll drums and play 'Dixie.'"

The place was packed and I came down through there with that T-shirt on... had more fun. I liked to dance my britches off that night.

... I always did wanna walk Waikiki Beach in my Miss Hatchie Bottom swimsuit, and I usually take a little something of Tuny with me when I go on a long trip.

When I walked into the lobby of the Hilton Hawaiian Village Hotel... "Good morning, Cuz"... to everybody... they looked at me real strange.

It so happened that the Dallas Cowboys, who had just won the Super Bowl that year, were down there on the beach playin' ball. They said "Well, hellooo."

"Hi, fellas. You know, this beach has to have one sex queen and here I am."

I had more fun cattin' around in the big sandbox... you make your own kind o' music. I am very fair, so I have to put lots of sunblock all over the body; the sun just bakes me to a little bitty black crisp. All these people were lyin' on their mats worshipping the sun. I'd lean over and say "'Mornin'. Ain't we havin' fun?" Had my teeth blacked out and the whole Tuny bit -- I bet I posed for a hundred pictures.

These people from all over the world were sayin' "They're not gonna believe this back home."

They have this bar called the Green Palm Room that opens out onto the beach... so the group I was with went in there for a drink and they got me up on the stage -- every afternoon we were there -- and I sang "Out Behind The Barn"... goin' out on loudspeakers all over that end of the beach in Hawaii. I had a hell of a time doin' it.

OUT BEHIND THE BARN

My pappy used to tan my hide

Out behind the barn

He taught me to be dignified

Out behind the barn

When he took his strap to me

And laid me down across his knee

He shor' did hurt my dignity

Out behind the barn

I smoked my first cigarette

Out behind the barn

And that's one day I won't forget

Out behind the barn

I got sick — you should have seen

How that tobacca turned me green

I darned near died from nicotine

Out behind the barn

I got my education

Out behind the barn

No, I ain't a-foolin', nossirree

Passed each examination

Out behind the barn

But it almost made a wreck out of me

I met a handsome boy one day

Out behind the barn

He asked me to stay and play

Out behind the barn

He taught me to kiss and pet

And that's one day I won't forget

'Cause we still play that same game yet

Out behind the barn

cuz

We went to a nightclub... and I was dressed normal that particular night. They asked me to sing with the band and I did. Invited me back on Friday night and I said "Okay. Tell ya what I'm gonna do. I'm gonna do the big act that I'm famous for stateside." I had a full-length, two-piece, cotton summer formal with long sleeves and a full skirt. I put my Miss Hatchie Bottom swimsuit on — the formal on top of it — and I walked into that nightclub. I sang a coupla numbers. Then I said "You guys know how to play 'The Stripper'?" They went "Uhhhhhhhhhhh" — started in with the drruuummmsss... I started unbuttonin' my blouse and everybody started screamin'. When I dropped that formal and was standin' there in the swimsuit, the place went bananas. They sold outta whiskey that night.

Miss Hatchie Bottom carried the torch in the 1990 Senior Olympics here in Jackson... hotter than the hinges of hell... running in front of the bleachers in Rothrock Stadium. Them little old people sittin' up there -- wild -- I thought, what am I doin' this for? But I was havin' a ball.

I mean it was hotter than a half-screwed sheep in a pepper patch. And, folks, you can't get much hotter than that.

Under the stadium I could hear one of 'em say... "Well now, what kind a' games are you gonna play today?"
Other one said "Well, I may play a little croquet and then I'm gonna do some Chinese checkers"...

I thought, we're talkin' about Gold Medal stuff here. Funny, funny people. I can talk about 'em because I'm there...

When I got my Medicare card... there're parts A and B... I called their office. This young girl answered the phone... its elevator didn't go to the top...

I said "I have graduated to Medicare and I have both parts A and B, and I wanna ask a question."

"Yes, ma'am."

"Does that cover pregnancy?"

There was dead silence.

I said "Are you there?"

"Oh, yes, ma'am. I guess if you got both parts, it do."

"I didn't say I had both parts for pregnancy, I just got both parts for Medicare."

"Well, okay, maybe you best see yo' doctor."

"Thank you very much." And I hung up. I just sorta needed to do that. Kinda helped me that day.

cuz

I'll probably end up on the front porch of a nursing home with my tongue hangin' out -- nyang-nyang-nyang -- and not be able to say a cottonpickin' word because I'd worn the mouth and vocal chords out, sittin' there in a wheelchair countin' the layaway tickets with a catheter in my bladder...

ALL MY OTHER CHILDREN

Thursday nights/"hospital" nights... when I'd visit the sick children and take them toys that I got from manufacturers... sometimes more than once a week when they would have indigent children and the nurses and doctors would call me to come out. Later on I started seeing the older people, too, and ended up visiting most everybody. I'd tell patients that they were wormy and I was going to de-worm them. I got a laugh from people who hadn't laughed in a long time. When they smiled, it did more for me than it did for them.

I always told the children, when they had to get a shot, to say "Cousin Tuny" ten times real fast and it wouldn't hurt as much. Sometimes the hallways would echo.

When you are from afar, people who were not native West Tennesseans visiting family members who were ill in the hospital, guess it was kind of a surprise to see somebody like me, in all my Tuny garb with my two front teeth blacked out.

One Thursday night I was paged to a particular nurses' station. They started laughing when I walked up.

"Tuny, this woman came flying down the hall a while ago. She said 'Oh, the worst thing has happened... I have to get my breath... I just ran up the steps.' We asked her why she didn't take the elevator and she said 'That's what I want to talk to you about. I started to get on the elevator and there was this woman in there with big ol' shoes on, teeth rotted out in front, sores all across her face... and she said "Come on in, youngun', the water's fine." Well, I wasn't about to get on that elevator. Do you know that someone from your psychiatric ward has escaped?!'"

CUZ

The nurses said "Don't worry about that. She's harmless. We just let her kinda roam around the hospital." I found the room where she was visiting and knocked on the door. A voice said "Come in."

I walked in and the woman said "Oh my God!"

The lady's daughter, who was laughing and holding herself from her surgery, said "I just told her about you." I said "Well, I want you to know you've hurt my feelings plumb down to my kneecaps. But I don't blame you. Had I been in your shoes, I wouldn't have gotten on the elevator with me either."

One day the nurses called me and said "This woman's wantin' to see you in there... she's got a nerve problem or somethin'."

So I went into the room and the woman said "Lord God, it's Cousin Tuny -- in person!"

"Cuz, you said you wanted to see me, and here I am."

Said "Lord, you look like you're fleshier and heavier set on the television ... why, you ain't as big as a bar of soap after a full day's wash. On the TV you look like you're about 80 years old. I bet you ain't a day over 50."

I was ready to put the pillow on that woman's face and start countin' slow to a hundred 'cause that was over 40 years ago, folks, and I was just in my thirties... made me feel so good.

I have a trophy case in my living room that houses items very dear to me. In there is a pin cushion, a little crocheted hat and two little hot pads with a little bit of crocheting around them, all handmade...

There was a hospital room back then that had four baby beds in it, like a ward. I walked in, and this woman was sitting there rocking a six-month-old baby who had a patch over both eyes. This was her grandbaby, and she said "Her mother is my daughter and she isn't worth killin'. She's run off, so looks like I'm gonna raise this baby. But the doctor said the baby would go blind if she did not have this surgery. I had to pay somebody to bring me up here." I looked over on the table and I saw candy bars lined up. It dawned on me that that's all this woman had to eat... that's what she'd been living on.

When I left I went to Georgia's Restaurant and told Georgia what had happened. I got some coffee and food that would be easily digested, and Georgia said she'd split it with me.

When I got back to the hospital, I went by Admitting and phoned the baby's surgeon, Dr. McIver. I said "Mac, that woman upstairs with the baby doesn't have any food... they said you would have to give the order for three regular meals a day and they'd charge it to me." He said okay.

It's a hell of a note when you think of all the food, and here is this lady trying to do what's right -- no money, no nothin', but she has got a lot of faith and a lot of backbone. She's the salt of the earth really.

Two of the Gray Ladies from the Red Cross, Callie Gurley and Juanita Conger, said they wanted to split it with me, so we did.

When I walked in with this food, the woman started crying... "Oh, Cousin Tuny..."

I said "Let me tell you something... you're going to have three meals a day as long as you're in this hospital. Don't worry about it. It's taken care of. I had a sick child once. And if you don't have food, you cannot withstand this. Just take care of that baby, that's the most important thing."

That was in late fall. When I went back the next week, they had gone. The baby had been dismissed.

About a week before Christmas I walked into the pediatric wing and the nurses said "We have something for you, Tuny. It was left here for you."

Those two little pot holders and that little-bitty hat, little-bitty pin cushion that she had made -- wrapped in tissue paper that had been used over and over and over again till it had been pressed... kind of a gray color... she put a straight pin in the top of it to keep it together. That's one of the finest presents I ever got in my life.

DIANNE AND MARK

Dianne O'Dell is in her fifties. When she was a little over three years old, she contracted Bulbar Polio and has been living in an iron lung since then. I often refer to Dianne when I am speaking to people. She graduated from high school with honors. She was connected electronically to the classes and used her foot to operate the switch. An honorary college degree was given to her by Freed Hardeman University in Henderson, Tennessee. Dianne can tell you what's going on in the Far East or just about anywhere in the world. "Blinky" is the title of a children's book written by Dianne. She autographed a copy for me by kissing it wearing lipstick.

She can move her legs, but that's all, and she can move her head from side to side... She's read most every book in the Jackson Library with a pencil in her mouth to turn the pages.

We raised some money, when I was at WJAK, and bought her some equipment that she can blow through a tube and answer the phone or dial the phone, turn TV off and on, change channels and turn lights off and on. So that gave her a little bit of independence. With the talking libraries, she has gotten a lot of novels on cassette that she can listen to, rather than have to read them because it's so difficult.

I asked her one time "Dianne, what is it that you think you've missed more than anything?"

"I don't ever remember putting my arms around my mother or my father or my sisters. I don't ever remember shaking hands with anybody, I don't remember reaching out and touching anybody."

"Yeah, but honey, you have a grip on everybody who's ever crossed your path that's unreal."

She's positive, she's very attractive and, after you go in that room, you only see that big old lung maybe four or five minutes 'cause you sit behind her, look in that mirror at that pretty, sweet face... and she's such a great conversationalist.

She has lived far longer than they ever thought she would. And that's just pure love because they are such a precious family.

Back in the early sixties, Mark was five years old and they found out he had leukemia. I would see him when they'd bring him for his blood transfusions and checkups with the doctor.

One night during the West Tennessee Fair I was in the Heart booth, for the Heart Fund, down under the grandstand in my pantaloons... I looked up and here came Mark in the wheelchair with his mother and daddy.

He said "I told 'em I'd be good, taking my blood and stuff today... if they'd just bring me down here and let me see you."

He was so bloated up, pitiful looking. He had this little ol' black and white plastic blown-up toy, and I said "Where'd you get that?"

"Well," he said, "I wanted the pink teddy bear, the big one, but Daddy just couldn't win it."

His father said "Tuny, I tried with all the money I had..."

I said "Why don't y'all roll in here in this booth and watch TV for a few minutes... I'll be right back... Would you stay till I get back?... Now, Mark, don't let 'em take you outta here till I return."

So here I go trompin' down through the midway.

I told the police "I'm gonna tell you somethin'... I've got to have one of those pink teddy bears... now if I grab one and run with it, I'll go to jail tomorrow, but I've got to have one of those."

Those people with the carnival, they'd see you in hell with your back broke; they wouldn't give you air if you were in a jug...

I had everybody around there throwing money tryin' to win a pink teddy bear... even some of the policemen.

A young man came around the corner with his arms full of teddy bears and stuffed animals that he had won. He said "Hey, Cousin Tuny."

I didn't know who he was, but I said "I need to talk to you about that pink teddy bear." And I told him about Mark.

He said "Oh, here, you can have it."

CUZ

"You come with me."

I was so excited when we walked up to Mark, and I said "Mark, see this young man here. He won this for you." And I handed him that pink teddy bear.

If you could have seen that little boy's face... kinda leanin' back in his wheelchair 'cause he couldn't sit up, he was so swollen.

Mark looked up at me and said "I just felt like you'd do something about this, Cousin Tuny."

About two weeks later, the Cisco Kid was on my TV show... it was Friday... I got him to autograph a picture for Mark and on Saturday morning I was called that Mark would like to see him. Well, Mark lived quite a distance and the Cisco Kid left town 30 minutes before I got to the motel.

I drove up to Mark's home... it was pouring down rain. Seems like every time somethin' like that happened, it was pouring down rain. My friend Ruth went with me. We carried that picture to Mark that Saturday morning and the little boy died within a couple of days.

Anyway, it made him happy. Had I gotten to the Cisco Kid in time, I'm sure he would have gone out there with me to see him 'cause he was a real nice guy. Oh me, such is life.

MINNIE PEARL

Minnie and I had more fun through the years, calling each other and tradin' jokes.

When she had a pacemaker put in, I sent her a card and wrote a note to remind her husband Henry... "Now that you are wired for 220 with that pacemaker, he needs to get his system checked 'cause he's liable to short-out... one plug-in and blam!"

Minnie called and we were talkin'... she said... "Tuny, Henry hasn't shorted out, but every time he kisses me the garage door goes up"... Then Minnie told me a couple jokes.

We went back and forth like that... then there's the one about... the old man goes home and says 'I've already bought our tombstone, double tombstone... go out at that cemetery and look at it... already got it inscribed on your side.' Old woman went out there and it said "Here Lies My Wife, Cold As Ever."

cuz

About two weeks later, she told him 'Go out and look at the tombstone, I've had your side inscribed.' So he went out there and it said "Here lies My Husband, Stiff At Last."

Minnie said she'd like me to come to Nashville and do a show with her at Vanderbilt Children's Hospital. I said I'd love it. So I drove to Nashville, met her and Henry for lunch, left my car and Henry carried us over to the Children's Hospital. I took my little red keyboard that I love dearly, and my pantaloons -- we dressed out -- had about 40 patients, children; and then the nurses and parents...

Minnie went out first and did some stuff for a few minutes. Then she said "Now I want to introduce my favorite cousin from Jackson, Tennessee, Cousin Tuny... come on out here, Tuny."

I went out with my keyboard and talked to the children and we sang... "She'll Be Comin' 'Round The Mountain" and "Let The Sunshine In" and a whole bunch of stuff. Then I looked down at these little black kids and said "You know how to rap?"

One little boy said "Uh-huh."

"Do you think I know how to rap?"

"Unh-unh."

"Well, I'm gonna show you." I turned around and said "Minnie Pearl, do you know how to rap?"

She said "What's that?"

"We're gonna have to make a cool cat out of my Cousin Minnie Pearl."

I hit that keyboard and I started rapping... "Hey, Mr. Whatcha callin', whatcha doin' tonight/ Oh, I hope you're in the mood 'cause I'm feelin' just right/ 'Cause I'm walkin' down the street and I love you, yes, sir/" And I went on, just makin' it up as I go... had great fun.

I presented a framed quote to Minnie and to the Children's Hospital where it hangs in their playroom:

"A hundred years from now nobody will remember who I was, what I did, or how much money I had. But the world may be a little different and a little better because I was important in the life of a child."

RUTH

"Life in the Mudholes"

Ruth had a wonderful life traveling with her husband, Jamie O'Neill, and their big band 'family' of 22 musicians before seeking a smaller town for their son Jimmy to grow up in. She became the widow-O'Neill and later married Bond Anderson, Jr., a marvelous and unique man. Their life was full of adoration and fun... she cared for him so lovingly. Ruth is the fairy godmother to my four children. They treasure her as much as I do.

She moved with Aaron Robinson, my brother-in-law, from The Jackson Sun, into the broadcasting business. "Mr. Robbie," as Ruth called him, was a workaholic and a master at any business deal he was involved in. He gave excellence and expected excellence in return... only then was he happy. Together they put radio, FM and a TV station on the air in a few short years.

That's when we met and became fast friends/ confidantes forever...

Aaron promoted wrestling matches at the old National Guard Armory; he sent Ruth and Slim Alexander to put up posters in store windows and on every telephone pole in West Tennessee. She was tying a poster on a pole and a woman with a rifle yelled "Get down off that pole!" With that, she took a shot at Ruth... Slim and Ruth both hit the car about the same time and scratched gravel gettin' outta there.

She was expert at 'screening' for Aaron and usually they communicated perfectly... then there were other times... Aaron had a few drinks and buzzed Ruth's desk... "If anyone wants to see me, tell them Agnes and I are on a cruise." A couple of salesmen came in wanting to see him and Ruth told them exactly what he had said. No sooner had she convinced them Agnes and Aaron were on a cruise than he opened his massive electric doors and staggered into her office — Ruth greeted him with "Hello, Mr. Robbie, when did you get back from your cruise?" "Cruise, cruise — hell, woman, I haven't been on any cruise; you're nuts!" The men looked at her sorta confused and quietly eased out the door, never to grace those portals again.

Our first time out — traveling to personal appearances — was an omen of years to come... We were sittin' there in my car, not talkative, unsure of what we'd gotten ourselves into... just ridin' down the road. All at once we saw this school with a lot of cars around it. I whipped in there; finally found a place to park. Everybody greeted us graciously. There were quilts hangin' everywhere and all kinds of crafts. Ruth announced "Ta-da!" with arms wide-spread — I went up on stage, sang a coupla numbers... then I looked around. Someone said "Gee, we have Cousin Tuny here... this is a great surprise!"

"Surprise? I was supposed to be here."

"Uh... well... no... uh..."

"What's the name of this school?"

We were in Lavinia, whatever that little school is up there in the mudhole... we were supposed to be in Clarksburg. 'Ta-dum' — — we tore out like two turpentined cats... laughing all the way... and only a little bit late to our real destination.

On our way to a school in Westport — it'd been pourin' down rain, muddy... Lord have mercy, never saw so much mud in my life. Ruth was dressed up fit to kill and I was in my best Tuny duds... lookin' great... had on the good boots and everything. Ruth wore a pair of beautiful alligator high-heels that she spent a year payin' out... She stepped out in that mud, and the next step she took... she didn't have a shoe on — standin' there barefooted, one-legged, the other leg just a-pumpin' around tryin' to find her shoe in the mud. It was pitch-black dark, you couldn't see your foot in front of your leg. There were a whole bunch of people there, so we had to park way down the road. Come to find out later, darn our luck, there was a place saved for us right by the door. Some fine gentleman picked her up bodily and carried her 'cause she couldn't walk. That was Ruth's brand-new shoe out there in that mudhole... and a year's worth of layaway.

We had this car sign that we put on top of my green Plymouth that had those big fins on the side... and that thing was anchored down... we thought. Huge sign — from the front to the back of that big four-door car — stood way up tall, in bright colors "COUSIN TUNY — HEART SUNDAY CHAIRMAN — FUNDRAISER FOR THE HEART FUND."

It was anchored to the corners of each bumper and to the door handles. We had no idea it was gonna be sleetin' and rainin' and the wind blowin' 70 miles an hour that day. It was a Sunday — and pretty soon we were gonna wish we were in church. Here we were, ridin' down the road, and that thing went "BOOMph" — it fell — we'd have to get out and tie it back up. We'd go a few more miles and it would fall the other way. We'd get out and put it right back up again. All in our furs and hats and high-heeled shoes. I imagine we were a sight on that highway that Sunday mornin'.

The sound of the rain was so loud we could barely hear each other speak. What we did hear was that sign goin' "GLLUU, GLLUU, GLLUU" and there it was again — it had suction cups, only the suction got slick and it didn't have any grip because the top of the car was so wet. Finally ended up takin' the blasted, cotton-pickin' thing off and put it inside — had a terrible time 'cause it was too big for the interior of the car. Part of it stuck out the back window — had to roll down the window — then we froze all the way.

People always seemed to think we had plenty of money, but we worked for peanuts — everybody did in those days. No cash; no money to spend. This particular Sunday I doubt if we had a quarter between us... tooling over to Brownsville for a Heart Association dinner in a very nice restaurant. We were sitting there enjoying our lovely meal when the bottom dropped out — The man at the head of the table got up and said "We've decided this is going to be a Dutch meal, everybody'll pick up their own tickets." Ruth and I looked at each other and our eyes glassed over... I could see me washing the dishes and Ruth mopping the kitchen floor. Thank heavens our friend Bob Allen came through... We were beginning to turn green around the gills as they brought the tickets. Bob said "I think I'll pick up these two ladies' tickets." I think he could tell that we were just about to leave this world.

American Heart held a meeting in New Orleans and we flew down... I entertained at the dinner. Afterwards they said "We're gonna take you down Bourbon Street." I said "Let me go change my clothes." "Aw, they won't pay any attention to you." There I was in my pantaloons. We went across Canal Street, got halfway across and almost stopped traffic.

We started down Bourbon and this fella was standin' out in the street hollerin' "Come see Miss Electra!!"... and there was this gal up there bumpin' and grindin' with a G-string on... this was in March and it was right chilly. I walked up and the guy said "My God, who are you?" "Mister, that woman in there's gonna catch her death o' cold 'cause she done took her long underwear off before the first day of May."

We went on down Bourbon Street and they took us to Antoine's for dinner. Sittin' there in the Tuny garb havin' a great time. Came the dessert course — they were doin' crepe suzettes. I looked up at the waiter with: "Do you know what happens to little boys who play with fire? They wet the bed." He turned around — dropped the dishes. When they brought the check, I inquired: "I wonder if you could cash my welfare check — I gotta have enough busfare to get back to Tennessee." This was at the beginning of open heart surgery, and the heart specialists who had been in concentrated discussions during dinner, created their own heart-stopping version of the E.F. Hutton commercial. Another moment in time.

Called to confirm our return flight... and we'd missed our plane. The tickets were nil, no good. There we were. Looked at each other like Lucy and Ethel on a bad-hair day... We could see ourselves thumbin' all the way from New Orleans back to Jackson. This was (yet another) Sunday mornin' and we had to be at work Monday mornin', or we'd both have gotten fired. Again, our friend Bob saved the day — scrounched us in his car; we were forever grateful.

When we came home we were hungry, but we didn't have any money. We'd lived off oysters and crackers all week while we were down there. We'd go to the Pearl Oyster Bar and split a dozen oysters, 55 cents a dozen, and they'd give us the po' boy bread; did that twice a day and that survived us. You can live on those things. I know 'cause we did. That and our little peanuts we had in the room with a Coca-Cola. That was it.

We had been at a program in Union City and it was very cold and late; spent the night in a motel in Fulton, Kentucky that was famous for their good food. We were gonna sleep late Sunday morning, have us a good breakfast before coming back to Jackson. The people in that motel looooooked at us — we knew they thought we were ladies-of-the-night hopin' for a place to make a little more money. We were pretty tired, but I didn't think we looked <u>that</u> bad. We almost didn't get a place to sleep... this was back in the days when you had to look nice... you couldn't drive up in jeans and big shirts like they do now and be accepted. Unh-unh.

After doing a show in Camden one night, we decided to stay in some sort of little lean-to in a tourist court. That motel room was the coldest... you could hang meat in there. We had one thin blanket on each bed — colder than Alaska. I think that was the coldest night I've ever spent in my life. And we had had rain upon rain upon rain upon sleet; and there must have been water in this room because the floor was wet; there wasn't a carpet; the wood was wet, even the bed felt like it was wet 'cause it was so cold.

We slept in our clothes. The next morning — they were

gonna give us a shortcut to Paris where we were doin' a radiothon fundraiser for the Heart Association. (That's Paris, Tennessee, folks; although France might have been quicker...) Here we go, headed out for the directions that some nerd gave us... My goodness alive, what a trip. First we knew we were lost because we came to the end of the road and there was the river. That wasn't the way to Paris. Backed up, turned around cautiously, surrounded by snow and ice. We were blazin' a new trail, no doubt about it. Ruth got out and went up to the front door of the only house for miles... she looked in the window, heard some commotion and sobbing. Lo and behold, Pa was dyin' — they were all over his bed cryin' and carryin' on — she sort of doodle-bugged back and off we took smack in the middle of no-man's-land.

We kept goin' and goin' and finally we ran out of road again. It just stopped. Backed up — took the other fork. Ruth said "See that house over yonder, Tuny?... stop and I'll go ask 'em if we can get to Paris on this road." Just as she got to the steps, my Lord, here came this vicious dog around the corner... Ruth made fast tracks back to the car yellin' "Open the door! Open the door!" I lit out like a bat outta hell; we were halfway down the road apiece before she could slam the door. Not exactly trippin' the light fantastic...

By the time we got to Paris — bull's-eye/bingo/ en-chalada — _how_ is a wonderment — they were already on the air; we blew into town in time for our appearance. That was one more trip.

We had to OD on PMA (overdose on positive mental attitude) to keep ourselves from getting bitter sometimes. We had our backs to the wall so much, we wore a hole in the corner.

But there _is_ life after mudholes. And we laughed — ohh — how we laughed...

"MORTGAGED PLYMOUTH"
Cuz Elvis Presley / Cuz Princess Margaret

About two years before Elvis died, I went to Las Vegas with Martha Armstrong. We stayed at the Circus Circus and had tickets down at the Hilton to see Elvis.

We looked like two wore-out prostitutes, I guess, dressed up in satin and furs and stuff... they don't really do a lot of that in Vegas.

Anyhow, we decided to walk to the Hilton. On that desert out there, you know what distance does to you. Everything looks like it's closer to you and it's way, way away. The more we walked, the further that hotel got. I was nearly dead by the time we got there.

I said "I'm gonna tell you one damn thing for sure... we are not walking back, my friend."

We go in and these people were waving hundred dollar bills... five hundred dollar bills... to get down on the ramp where Elvis comes out and throws scarves and stuff. Martha said, "We'll be put in the pigeon roost."

I said "Just watch me."

I walked up to the maitre d', handed him a ten dollar bill and said "'Scuse me, sir, but I ain't never seen Cousin Elvis do his numbers on the stage and we done got dressed up here to come out here and see him."

He said "Are you from Tennessee?"

"Yes, sir, I live up the road thar apiece from Cousin Elvis."

He had them take us to this table that was on the first level and we were about twenty feet from the end of the ramp he came out on.

The word started passing around that Elvis Presley's cousin was sittin' there.

Martha said "Now what in the hell are you gonna do?"

"I don't know."

Some guys and gals came out and did the warmup for him, and then here comes Elvis. Everybody's screamin'... the women are fallin' out...

Poor man, he was so bloated, looked like he was going to explode... within the 45 minutes he was onstage, he drank twenty glasses of water. I knew then, man, he wasn't spittin' cotton.

When he sang the American Trilogy and went into the part that says 'Oh, I wish I was in the land of cotton'... I stood up and went "Yeeeeeehooooooooo!"

Elvis looked up and everybody looked at me; I threw him a kiss and he threw me a kiss back. He didn't know me from Adam.

This woman sittin' at the next table, some Yankee, was lookin' at me.

I said "Lady, I don't know about you, but that's my National Anthem he started singin' then, that's 'Dixie,' y'all."

I got outta that one.

"Welfare Cadillac" was popular on a 45 rpm in '69, I believe it was...

This song I kept hearing kinda got to me. I felt it went

against the grain of us 'working-class heroes.' So I decided to answer it with another song.

I came home, took my uke and went out in my garage-turned-studio, wrote and taped my song, which is actually spoken.

I took it back to the radio station, and the next day Curtis White, on his early morning show, said "Ladies and gentlemen, we have an answer to 'Welfare Cadillac.' Cousin Tuny's done this, she says, for all the working people out there. I'm gonna play 'Welfare Cadillac' first and follow it with 'Mortgaged Plymouth.'"

MORTGAGED PLYMOUTH

I live in a house with a mortgage today

That'll last 20 years, but I intend to pay

From my earnings I work for day by day

Now I don't get a check from the government

But my taxes increased, and the money I've spent

To try and pay my way and my children's through school

Yet there's some folks seem to think that --

That I'm just a fool

I buy my own groceries, slowly by the sack

Don't get no commodities, so don't own no Cadillac

cuz

But I have got a Plymouth, and it's financed too

And I make them bank payments from the work that I do

Ah, my budget is hurtin', an' to help make ends meet

I soak them beans longer so we'll have more to eat

But I'm thankful I'm able to make my own way

An' I'll keep driving my Plymouth an' workin' every day

But it does set you to thinkin' when you try an' try

And you look up and see a new Cadillac glide by

Full o' youngun's and commodities, all livin' for free

On the taxes and hard work by you and me

So Mr. President, I'd like you to take just a minute

And play this little message to the United States Senate

Now I ain't really complainin' or pollutin' the air

I just wanna ask

Do you think it's fair?

    Well, the phones began to ring off the wall and Paul Harvey closed out his newscast the next day on ABC with my "Mortgaged Plymouth."

    A reporter from the <u>Commercial Appeal</u> newspaper in Memphis interviewed me about the song and the story hit the Associated Press wire.

I cut the record and Jimmy Exum, who was producing it, said "You gotta have somethin' for the other side." So that's when I wrote the lyrics and music for "Yes-sir-ee Bob-o-link-o." The phrase was a favorite with the children on TV...

YES-SIR-EE BOB-O-LINK-O

When you're feelin' blue
  And you don't know what to do
  And you fall and stump your toe
The magic word is 'Yessiree'
'Yessiree Bobolinko'

First you pick yourself up, up real quick
Brush yourself off, ah, it ain't no trick
Just make up your mind and stay on the go
With a great big smile
And 'Yessiree Bobolinko'

Now it's not too easy when you wake
And look yourself in the mirror
  Oh, what a sight, but things'll look bright
When you make that smile grow nearer

CUZ

And every time you have a bad day

This one thing I know

Everything'll look up if you smile and say

'Yessiree Bobolinko'

(It's magic, Cousin) 'Yessiree Bobolinko'

(Smile now) 'Yessiree Bobolinko'

(All day long) 'Yessiree Bobolinko' (Keep it up)

I sent a tape of "Mortgaged Plymouth" to President Nixon and got a letter back from the gal who erased the Watergate tapes... at least he heard it.

Right after cutting the record, I was on my way to Europe for the first and only international meeting of American Women in Radio and Television. I'd scraped and skinnied to go.

I signed a contract with BMI in London because the rep happened to be on the trip and she had the contract with her.

"Mortgaged Plymouth" was being aired in 42 states and, wouldn't you know, it runs in the family, this kind o' luck... it was going great... I guess I made three or four hundred dollars from it... the last check I got was for somethin=few cents... I framed it 'cause I figured it'd probably be the last one I got from BMI.

We were in Sligo, Ireland and I walked into the lobby of the little hotel that had one TV set. They were announcing that we had marched into Cambodia.

I turned around to the gals I was with and said "Forget 'Mortgaged Plymouth'"... because anything that was controversial like that -- died right quick on the vine.

I think the recording company went kaput, bankrupt... the label is as dead as the record is... but I'm glad I did it. I'm a recording star... hoppity-toppity.

In London, the record people said "We may need to call you, so when you check in at the hotel, be sure to tell them you're expecting a call from the States because sometimes they're kinda slow at getting people to the phone."

So after I registered at the Royal Garden Hotel... had my Cousin Tuny badge with professional identification... I walked up to the desk clerk and said "I am Doris Freeman, in room 741, and I am expecting a very important call from the States."

He said "Oh, I say, you are an entertainer, aren't you?"

"Well, after a fashion."

"Oh, after a fashion?"

You know, they take everything you say literally.
He said "If you get a call from the States, I shall personally come round and knock you up."

"I beg your pardon?!"

There happened to be an American woman standing behind me. She said "Tuny, that means 'look you up' over here."

"But it sure don't mean that in Madison County."

For the next two weeks, everybody said "Hey, Tuny, you been knocked up yet?"

"Nope. Left the door open, not a soul. Story of my life."

CUZ

During introductions to an Englishman, I said "It's good to see you."

He said "Keep your pecker up."

I was told "That means keep your chin up."

"It don't mean that in Madison County either."

AWRT had a big party at Lancaster House and Princess Margaret was there... I bathed twice that day... she's a swinger, my kind of folks. I did the royal squattin' -- they call it the curtsey, but I call it the royal squat.

VICKS SALVE

A Caribbean cruise is terrific. You get away from people, the food is fantastic, and there're all sorts of things to do.

We were on the S.S. Emerald Seas out of Miami. Beautiful ship. I shared a cabin with Marge Lee, who arranged the trip.

One night I was propped up in bed to read and I said "Will this reading bother you, with the light on?"

She said "No."

So I was reading and she was over there snortin' and carryin' on, and I said "Marge, are you having problems breathing?"

"Yeah, I am."

"You want some Vicks salve?"

"I don't believe you have brought Vicks salve on a Caribbean cruise."

"Hey, I don't go anywhere without the Vicks salve."

She said "Yeah, I do"...

She took it and put some in her nose and wiped her hand off with a Kleenex. Then she said "Now I've got to go to the bathroom."

She goes into the bathroom... comes back. All of a sudden, when she sits down on the bed, she says "Oh my

God, I used that Kleenex that I wiped my hand with the Vicks salve."

She had wiped her bottom with it. Now you're talkin' about somethin' funny... She did a dance like I've never seen before. I mean, she was doing the Vicks Salve Shakes And Shimmies...

She ended up going to get a bath cloth and put it in cold, cold water and sat on it.

So if you ever use Vicks salve, be sure you don't use it on the south end.

I told her "Now you know what a turpentined cat feels like."

MISS TEOLA

Over in Trezevant, Tennessee lived a cute little old lady -- Miss Teola Dunlap. She wrote a column "Trezevant Route 2" for the Carroll County newspaper.

People from all over the country would subscribe to that paper just to read that column because they never did edit it. They printed it exactly like she wrote it. She would say "I was on the party line... now, mind you, I did not mean to listen in, but I was on the party line and I heard... there's four parties on my line... I heard Sophie talkin' to Danny..." and she'd tell all the gossip. It was funny.

I was at a football game as Tuny up in Bruceton, appearing for the Heart Fund. Governor Gordon Browning was there, and he was always surrounded by Highway Patrolmen...I was standing there talking to them and we got on the subject of newspapers. I said "You know, there's one somebody I would love to meet, and that's Miss Teola Dunlap who writes 'Trezevant Route 2.'"

One of the Patrolmen said "Tuny, I want to be the one to introduce you to Miss Teola. I know her, and she's exactly like the column she writes. She lives out in the country from Trezevant."

That next February I was in Trezevant in my pantaloons at a basketball game for the Heart Fund. All of a sudden, here comes this Highway Patrolman, picks me up bodily off the court and says "You're under arrest!" And carries me outside, puts me in the squad car.

He got in and said "Now we're gonna go meet Miss Teola.

You didn't want to stay in there anyway, did you?"

I said "Oh, I certainly want to meet Miss Teola."

It was cold, God, colder'n a well-digger's bottom in January in Iowa with no seat covers on him... So we went way out in the country. You couldn't see your hand in front of you, it was so pitch-black dark.

Pulled up at this little country house, porch all the way across the front, kinda beshackled.

He said "You stay here in the car."

He left the lights on and went up and knocked on the door. Shouted back "She's here, Tuny."

I got out, went up on the porch, the door opened, and there she stood. Miss Teola had little-bitty kid curlers all over her head, hair rolled up in them. She had a coal oil lamp in her hand, had on its good housedress and apron, sort of a frumpy-looking woman...

She said "Lord God, it's Cousin Tuny comin' to my home. How'd I ever get this honored? Come on in. Come on through the front room."

We went on through... it was cold as kraut in the front room.

Said "Back here in the middle room's where we have the far (fire)."

We went in and sat down -- the house smelled like pine knots and coal oil.

She said "We been poppin' some corn."

There sat this young teenaged girl and a young man.

Miss Teola said "This is my daughter Kathleen. This is

Aaron (she said Erin) -- and they're gonna get married."

I said "Oh, how nice."

"Oh, Cousin Tuny, I wanna do a column on you. Do you mind?"

"I'd be flattered."

"Oh, I've never been so honored in all my life."

She was such a dear lady...

She said "I've got to find my tablet to write on."
She couldn't find the tablet. All she could find was the back of a tablet 'cause all the pages were out. So she took the pencil, touched the lead on her tongue --

"This is so it'll write darker, so I can see better, see" -- and poised to write on the cardboard back of the tablet.

The next week when the paper came out, well, you'd have thought that St. Peter had come to visit her. It was a beautiful thing.

The very next week, she told about Kathleen gettin' married. She said "Now Kathleen and Aaron got married in the front room over in one corner. The Pastor came and married 'em. And Aaron was wearin' a white short-sleeve sport shirt." And that's all she said he was wearing... I'm sure he was wearing something else, but that's all she said.

"Kathleen was wearin' a white dress. And after the ceremony, everybody went over to a' other corner of the front room where the table was and everybody had a slice of cake and a saucer of cream." (That means a saucer of ice cream.)

Miss Teola was quite a character. About five or six months

after that, I was in Trezevant making a personal appearance at the one big department store -- the Dry Goods Store -- with Kedso the Clown, on behalf of Keds. There were a ton of people there. I don't know where all those people and children came from. I was signing autographs when I looked up, and over in the corner was Miss Teola. People around there sorta made fun of her...

I said "Oh, there's my friend Miss Teola Dunlap. You get over here, Miss Teola." And I went over and hugged her neck.

She said "Oh, thank you. Nobody's ever paid attention to me before like that."

"HELLO DOLLY"

Speaking of fine ladies, I saw Mary Martin portray Dolly Levi in "Hello Dolly" many years ago in Memphis. She just mesmerized me, and I sat there like I'd treed a possum.

At the last curtain call, Ms. Martin told this story... She was in her dressing room and there came a knock on the door. It was Oscar Hammerstein who was the musical's lyricist. He put a crumpled piece of paper in her hand and said "You inspired me to write this passage of lyrics in the score of 'The Sound of Music' because I think you're such a fine lady." She kissed him on the cheek and said "Oh, thank you so much." And he left. Then she heard the stage manager's 'places' call, put the paper in her dressing gown pocket, hung the gown on the costumer, and went onstage for her performance.

At the end of the show, the cast was called together and told that Mr. Hammerstein had terminal cancer. Ms. Martin related, "I ran to my dressing room, over to my costumer, reached in the pocket of my dressing gown and pulled out this crumpled piece of paper. He had written these words:

'A bell is not a bell until you ring it

A song is not a song until you sing it

Love was not put in your heart to stay

And it is never real love until you give it away.'"

I was so impressed that night I watched her. My friend Ruthie was with me, and on the way home we talked about the experience...

I said "You know, that's always been one of my

dreams, to play Dolly Levi."

Ruth said "Well, you would be perfect for the part."

"I don't know about that, but I would sure like to try it; and if I ever have the chance, I'll close my performance with that quote and tell about Mary Martin."

As fate would have it, I did play Dolly at the Civic Center...

The night of dress rehearsal I had a unique thing happen to me. The cast were all in opening costumes, and we had an audience that night... the Civic Center was about half-full and roped off, with the tech crew working on the lights...

I had a microphone in my bra with the backpack underneath my girdle. And it was the first time that I had used it. I was onstage... singing "Hello, Harry, well, hello, Louie"... we were checking the system being controlled from the sound booth.

They said "Okay, Tuny, everything's fine, sound level's good."

So I sat down, waiting for us to begin the rehearsal... we were going through the show nonstop and Dolly Levi's onstage so much of the time... I thought I'd better ease out and go to the little girls' room and partake of the facilities because I wouldn't get another chance... Got into one of the stalls and pulled all that long dress and stuff up, pulled my seat covers down and got myself seated on the throne and started my participation.

Here came this gal through the door screamin' "Tuny, Tuny, your mike is on and it sounds like Niagara Falls is coming through the Civic Center!!"

I confessed into my mike: "Well, ladies and gentlemen, I am sorry but I cannot stop this horse in the middle of a stream."

I had to do something, you know, there I sat, I couldn't stop!

She said "Are you going back out there?"

"Is the Pope Catholic? Of course I'm going back out there."

I walked through the door with "Ta-da!" The place went bonkers. Everybody was in the floor.

cuz

SYMPHONICALLY YOURS

On the Jackson Symphony Orchestra's slate was "Porgy and Bess."

Mr. Petty, the Conductor, asked me to be a guest artist because there was a marimba in the score.

I said "Now Mr. Petty, I don't think -- "

"Just come to rehearsal."

So I went... Oh Lord, I should never have gone in the first place.

I went up on the stage and there were all those legitimate musicians, and there I was, the only illegitimate musician in the bunch... walked up behind this four-and-a- half octave marimba (mine is two-and-a-half octave)... and they laid all this music out in front of me written in five flats; they were 16th notes.

Now you have to turpentine the mallets with that sort of time and 16th notes. As I've mentioned, I don't read music... like the monkey on the pickle barrel, you hum it and I'll try to play it.

Mr. Petty took his baton and hit on the side of the music stand; said "Ladies and gentlemen, Cousin Tuny is here to rehearse with us -- possibly to do a solo at the next symphony concert."

Everybody hit on their little violins and their little doo-dads.

I thought, Oh God, yeah, I'm gonna play so low you can't hear me.

Mr. Petty continued "We'll begin, and at the andante vivo --"

I thought, Shut my mouth. I looked down there, it said a-n-d-a-n-t-e v-i-v-o there on the music.

He said " -- and then we'll play 16 bars."

I thought, After 16 bars, hell, I can play all the instruments in this orchestra.

They start -- I'm about six bars down the path and, all of a sudden -- they quit.

I looked up and said "Are y'all through? Maybe I better take this home with me and look at it."

I picked up the music and out I walked... just as flushed as I could be...

In reading music, I have to go with the treble... Every Good Boy Does Fine and F-A-C-E for the spaces. For the bass it's Good Boys Do Fine Always and All Cows Eat Grass...

So I brought it home. And I had my son Jim, who was in the school band under Mr. Petty's direction, take the music back and tell him that I just couldn't make it.

I was replaced by a twelve-year-old boy.

That's about as symphonic as I get...

JOHN

I have a little den that is absolutely loaded with framed pictures on the walls... from day one. My children tell me, come the earthquake, <u>do not</u> be in this room.

There is one particular photo amongst the masses that means so very much to me. A little boy, John, Santa Claus, me as Tuny, and the young woman who was his mother. I had another one just like it hanging on my office wall. There's a special story behind that picture...

In December, 1960, that boy was five years old and he was due to appear on my TV show. The night before he was to be on television with the group of his friends, Nancy, his mother, was bathing him and found a knot in his stomach. The next morning she carried him to the doctor and John was immediately hospitalized. They did surgery and told the parents that he had a malignancy.

It was Christmas Eve -- John was in the hospital and they were going to let him go home for Christmas. He knew that Santa and Tuny were coming to the hospital, so they waited until we got there before leaving.

Every Christmas Eve, for so many years, we held a pancake breakfast at Fox Restaurant, when downtown Jackson was booming with businesses. They had some gifts and toys that people sold chances on... all the money went to the Cancer Society. That year they decided to send those toys out to John. And that's what he's doing in the picture, looking at the gifts with me and Santa.

Beginning at that time... they sent a copy of the picture to me and I put it on television.

I told John on TV "I'm gonna hang this picture of you and me and Santa in my office."

From that time until he died, in July of '61, I saw John at least once a week, most of the time, twice a week. I'd just bop by the house to say hello. And every day on TV I dedicated one of the cartoons ("Cartunies") to John.

We had this little thing we went through every time I went by...

He'd take my hand and sometimes I'd hold him in my lap and he would say "What am I?"

I'd say "John, you're my very extra special little cousin."

"I love you, Cousin Tuny."

"I love you, John."

And I'd kiss him on the forehead.

His sixth birthday was May 13th. He wanted to have his birthday party on my show, and we made sure that happened. I alerted my staff and all the cameramen that this would not be easy for me.

When I walked into the studio before the show, he was there. That small pale beautiful face... he had on a white sailor suit with short pants... he looked up at me and started smiling... such a drawn look, and that distended abdomen...

I knelt down, he put his arms around me and said "I want to see your room."

"Okay, we have time."

I carried him back to my office... he looked around the walls. I knew what he wanted. The picture, of course, was hanging on the wall.

He said "Cousin Tuny, will you sit down in your chair, please?"

"Yes."

"Now will you lift me up in your lap?"

And I did.

He put one hand on one side of my face and one hand on the other, looked straight in my eyes with those big brown eyes and long lashes -- God, I'll never forget it -- "Cousin Tuny, will my picture always hang on your wall?"

I said "Always."

"No matter what happens?"

"No matter what happens, John. That's a promise."
He put his arms around me and said "I love you, Cousin Tuny."

In July I was called and they had carried John to the hospital.

When I walked in, one of the nurses said "Tuny,

he's going to die this time."

That little fellow was up under an oxygen tent, already had the death grunt, abdomen so distended it looked like he was going to burst.

Lying beside him was a white rifle, a Kadet rifle -- the first one that came off the production line at Parris Manufacturing Company in Savannah, Tennessee. I stood there as the first one was assembled for him and Cecil Parris, God rest his soul, said "I want that boy to have this."

There was also a Bugs Bunny I'd given him on the bed.

CUZ

He wanted to carry those things with him to the hospital.

We went through our little thing and he said "What am I?" in between his groans.

"You're my extra special little cousin."

"I love you, Cousin Tuny."

"I love you, John."

That little frail hand came out from under the oxygen tent. And when I grabbed ahold of that hand, I had ahold of the hand of God because that was a dying six-year-old child in pain.

He looked up at me, and the kicker was, he said "Oh, Tuny, my bones hurt."

There I stood... a great big grown somebody... and I could not do anything for him.

That little boy has raised a good bit of money since I've told his story at charity events and telethons; and, believe me, it's a difficult story to tell...

I told John goodbye and that I loved him and I left. At the very end, I knew that his mother and father should be alone with him.

The next morning about seven o'clock my phone rang and his father said "Tuny, John quit hurting last night about fifteen minutes after you left."

In 1972 I was called at 2:30 in the morning by Aaron, Jr. that WDXI was on fire and that an explosion had just gone down through my office and blown everything to bits -- 25 years of work.

First thing I thought about when I hung up the phone was,

my picture burned... I didn't think about all those plaques and things that couldn't be replaced; but, thank God, nobody was up there when lightning struck that building.

At 7:30 that morning I called John's mother and said "Nancy, my picture burned."

She said "I have another one."

It was replaced and I had several made from it so I would have copies. I look at that picture often and it makes a better person of me. I leaned on that little boy through the hard last months before my sister's death; she died a month after John. He was my rod and staff.

It's amazing how much strength you get from people that you don't realize you would. It was quite an incident in my life that humbled me and wrung my heart out at the same time.

AGNES

Letting Go

When she was 36, Agnes began to lose weight and she was eating like crazy... especially candy. We took Pat, Cindie, Jim and Connie to the Strawberry Festival Parade in Humboldt and she ate a bunch of candy bars and couldn't get enough to drink.

Within the next few days, she ended up in Fitts-White Clinic under Dr. Burrus, Sr.'s care... they found out she had sugar diabetes and was about to go into a diabetic coma. She had to take a shot of insulin every day and was supposed to watch her diet.

My sister had her own personal problems at that time, too, so her physical condition didn't make life any easier for her. To me she was the Rock of Gibraltar and I felt like nothing would ever happen to her.

She had always had bronchial problems and, when she was about 44 years old, she began to worsen... building fluid... gaining weight...

She had a good-lookin' figure; tall, like Daddy, and had that smooth walk and gorgeous, sexy ankles. She was so beautiful outside and inside...

They found out that her heart was enlarged when she started building fluid. She was hospitalized and they put her on fluid pills and adjusted her sugar level. It was an off and on thing like that from then on.

She slept under oxygen the last year of her life... at that time it was a big tent. She had a nurse in the daytime, and I would stay a lot at night with her... I'd go out late after the children were in bed; and if I had to speak or perform somewhere, I'd leave early in the morning. You wonder sometimes how you get through things like that.

All through the years with Agnes' illness I was active in the West Tennessee Heart Association... Every time I would perform for them I'd close by talking about Agnes... telling everybody that, if you don't have a personal reason, you will have, because heart disease is the number one killer in the world.

There was a hospital in Humboldt at the time called St. Mary's. Sister Mary Blandine was the Administrator... she was delightful.

Sister Mary told me she would like to visit Agnes. She and Sister Emiliana, another nun stationed there, both wanted to come. And Agnes said she'd love to meet them.

cuz

Tommy Lee was the houseboy... an African-American boy mentored by Agnes when he was twelve years old — gave him a home and taught him how to clean and scrub and polish and serve. He just loved her. She was his white momma and he was her black child.

He was running the vacuum cleaner up and down the hall. Ms. Hamlet, Agnes' nurse, had come downstairs when the doorbell rang. It was Sister Mary Blandine and Sister Emiliana, in their white habits.

Hamlet put them on an elevator that had been installed during the illness, and said "This will stop right outside Mrs. Robinson's door and you just go on in, she's expecting you. I'll fix us some tea and bring it up."

Hamlet said that she was in the kitchen fixing the tea, and here came Tommy Lee flyin' down the back stairs. He looked right gray; lost his black.

He said "Oh, come quick, come quick, Ms. Hamlet. Two angels done come up there after Ms. Robinson! Come on quick, we don't want her to go yet. <u>Come on</u>!"

Ms. Hamlet got so tickled because the boy had never seen Catholic nuns. He was running the vacuum in the hall upstairs when that elevator slowly came up and there were those two women in white habits.

One of the times Agnes was in the hospital... it was about two o'clock in the morning and I was sitting there, as they kept comin' in and comin' in because her pulse was getting weaker and weaker... and I was praying, Oh God, please don't let her die now. Of course love is selfish and I didn't realize how selfish I was being. She was so miserable.

The nurses called the doctor in; and, all of a sudden, he looked at me and said "Hey, her pulse is getting stronger."

Agnes opened her eyes, looked at me and started smiling. She said "Oh, Tuny."

"Don't talk now."

"Oh Tuny, I've got to tell you something. I just had the most beautiful dream and I want to tell you about it."

The doctor said "Let her tell you."

I got close and she said "I dreamed that I was barefoot and I was standing on all this green grass that felt like velvet. It was beautiful. I looked up and saw these lights and I heard the most beautiful music I've ever heard in my life... this gorgeous choir and chorus singing 'The Hallelujah Chorus.' Oh Tuny, it was just beautiful. All of a sudden, a voice said 'Agnes.' I turned and all I could see was just a form. 'Agnes, take my hand.' I said "Oh no, I don't want to miss a bit of this music.' Then I woke up."

I looked at her and said "Well, we're gonna have to get you some more 'Hallelujah Chorus' pills."

For the next year that she lived, we'd say "We wanna have 'The Hallelujah Chorus' dream tonight..."

About two weeks before she died, we went downstairs to get some dill pickle and peanut butter and crackers... she could have anything she wanted at this point.

I fixed the tray to take back upstairs and we shuffled through the butler's pantry, into the dining room and she said "Stop here a minute, Tuny. Look down that hall. This is a magnificent house, a beautiful home. We have Oriental rugs everywhere, gold-leaf furniture, hand-carved dining room furniture, solid cherry, everything. In the garage is a brand-new

Cadillac and a brand-new Lincoln. But look at me, Tuny." And she held her hand up... "It's not worth the snap of your finger -- because you see, you're the rich one and I'm the poor one, because what you've got money can't buy."

I thought I was going to break up, but I bit my lip and said "Well, don't you tell my creditors that I'm so rich."

She said "Oh, you fool you."

... It was a Sunday afternoon when Agnes went back to the hospital for the last time. She would come and go... so swollen and so full of fluid... her thighs were as big as my hips and the fluid was oozing out of the pores of that lady's skin on her legs. God, it was awful. She didn't deserve that; she never hurt a flea in her life. I reached down and kissed her on the lips. They were clammy and cold. I took her hand and she opened her eyes. I used to call her "tuiter" when I was little because I couldn't say sister.

"I love you, tuiter."

When she died, she turned around to Ms. Hamlet and said "Hamlet, hold me up, help me up." She was almost in a sitting position because she couldn't breathe with all that fluid.

Agnes held out her hand, and she was gone. That quick. Sister Mary and Sister Emiliana walked up to the casket; Sister Mary put her arm around me and said "Honey, think about this now. As much as she loved you, she wouldn't come back if she had the chance."

And you know, that lifted a weight off my shoulders like you wouldn't believe. They wouldn't come back if they had the chance. Why would they wanna come back into all this? They don't have any more problems.

That's why, when I die, I want a big celebration 'cause

I'll be through. I will have finished. Until I'm reincarnated into somethin'. Lord knows what the next life will be.

It was like burying another mother because she was like my mother, my buddy and my pal; and her influence on my life has been great. Every day I think about her.

JENNY

"Jenny, you better get here if you wanna see Agnes alive."

That's the call I had to make to our sister Jenny in North Carolina, shortly before Agnes succumbed. She and her husband Bill came and she stayed with Agnes for four or five nights. The last night we all stayed together. But I wanted Jenny to spend time with her. When they arrived Jenny said, "Oh Doris, I don't think I can do this."

I took her hand and said "Now you've got to keep it together. That's what you've got to do."

We went up and Agnes said "I want each of you to sit on either side of me." She put her arms around us and said "This is the last time we'll all three be together on earth. But I'm gonna see Mother and Daddy. I just wanted you to sit here a few minutes with me."

I reached around and started pinchin' on Jenny, for fear that she was going to fall apart, but she held it together. And she told Agnes goodbye.

She held it until she got outside, and she was a basket case when she left. When Bill drove her down the driveway, she was all but screaming. I really felt for her...

It seemed like slow motion, with all the intense love in the air, as I watched them drive away... I started thinking of Jenny... and years and years and years ago...

Mother used to wake me on New Year's Eve when the bells would ring. It was a big thing -- you could hear bells ringing and guns going off and fireworks all over town.

She'd hold me real close and say "Doris, Santa Claus is on his way back to the North Pole, and you've been such a good little girl, he just might leave you a surprise on his way back."

I'd slide back down in that big old feather bed and go back to sleep.

On New Year's morning, there would be a gift there for me. It was usually something I'd asked for but didn't get. I figured later on that they had probably run out of money and it was on sale, but not always. And it was invariably something that I wanted real bad. It was such a dear thing to do...

Jenny carried on that tradition until she passed away. She'd send me a gift every year... it might be a little stuffed animal or a little-bitty somethin' with candy sticks in a shoe box.

"Santa was on his way back to the North Pole and he dropped this by, so I told him I'd send it on to you."

We almost lost Jenny when she was a teenager... it was before Mother became seriously ill.

I was seven years old when Jenny contracted double pneumonia and she was sick for two years. She was in the front bedroom when I went in to see her. Jenny told me that night "See that little cobweb on the ceiling..." (which was unusual 'cause our mother was an immaculate housekeeper)... "If that cobweb falls, Doris, I will die."

I said "Well, it's not gonna fall because I'm gonna pray and it isn't gonna fall."

The night the ambulance came to take her to the hospital... back then, this was 1932... the yard was full o' people... an ambulance was coming and all the neighbors from everywhere

cuz

came around.

They took her to Webb-Williamson Hospital, which is now a parking lot next to First Methodist Church on Chester Street. Dr. Webb did surgery. They went into her back, sawed out one of her ribs and drained her lungs. She was a very sick young lady. In fact, she was in a wheelchair and had to learn to walk again.

Slowly, Jenny recuperated over the next two years and I used to go with her to Dr. Brown's office downtown -- the same "Brown" as my middle name. (That's what you got when they ran out of names and you're the runt of the litter.)

They would put this ultraviolet somethin' on her back, and she had to wear this tube in her back for drainage.

I loved to get her tickled... that thing would sputter and spew out her back... She got through it...

CHRISTMASTIME!!

Mother loved Christmas; and, consequently, I love Christmas... from as far back as I can remember.

These years it's the only time we get to be together, my four children, from Los Angeles to South Carolina, four grandsons, great-grandson, and significant others.

So my house is far from quiet during Christmas week. It's such a time of celebration and laughter... I get to where I just ain't worth killin'.

I zip to the grocery store and buy things I never would normally. One Christmas, in anticipation of all my chicks bein'-to-home, I really loaded up my shopping cart... buying everybody's favorite foods. Got home -- searching for another inch to cram the stuff into the refrigerator and cabinets -- got to the bottom of the last bag -- cat food. No... I do not have a cat. What can I say?!

My house is small and I have enough memorabilia collected to make a cleaning woman with a dust rag request a transfer to the Smithsonian. The decor is "early clutter." But it's Tuny clutter and I like it -- people don't like it, they don't have to come back -- however, for some reason, they do return.

I suppose the pure sophistication of it all is underwhelming and must be my drawing power.

The sitting/standing situation at Christmastime kinda boggles the mind. Beaucoups of food surrounded by a plethora of Xmas decorations... stockings for everyone; mine, natch, being a high-button shoe... the Christmas tree holds some precious ornaments made by my TV and hospital children.

The garage-turned-studio-turned-"Tuny Motel" houses a few relations. Since I can't buy my way to Bemis on the bus with a transfer, I figure, push comes to shove, I'll start taking MasterCard and rent it out by the hour... maybe on a percentage basis.

Now, there really isn't enough room for the twenty-some-odd persons lounging in my holiday consortium. Just how it works out remains one of those little mysteries in life that we are not here to question.

One particular year comes to mind -- ohmigod -- was it freezing! Ice everywhere and not a drop to drink... the plumbing froze... pipes burst in the ground... and there we all were. The city had to come out -- ripped open the snow/ice-covered yard to get to the pipes -- and all this muck and slush and gunk started spewing all over the place. It was crazy... all of this with the phone ringing intermittently hollerin' Xmas love calls from Jenny, my niece Carol, nephew Sonny (Aaron Jr.), and myriad friends of the fam.

Jim and Cindie went to get "Ludy" Tillman who lived just a couple streets over. She brought her zither and played for everybody in her inimitable fashion. I joined in with my keyboard and we had a big ol' time. Ludy never did lose her infectious laugh since our "tour" of Sweet Lips, Tennessee... She is sorely missed.

My dear friend Oller scooted by... Oller always reminded me of Tugboat Annie, quite a character, and good as gold. She made mouth-watering divinity and heavenly boiled custard for me every year, and an incredible German chocolate cake that she knew was a favorite with Cindie and Connie. Oller and her sister Virtis were like the Snoop Sisters -- nothing like a trip taking them to dinner and thoroughly enjoying their cantankerous banter -- amusing and sweet.

I took time every year to visit the hospital children, in my "Christmas" Tuny garb, with Santa Claus.

This song I wrote for Santa:

SWINGIN' SANTA

Well, everybody loves the big fat man with
the beard in the bright red suit

Everybody loves the big fat man
'cause he gives away that loot

On Christmas Eve he takes a trip
across the sky, you see

He does his thing and makes us sing
around the Christmas tree

Yes, everybody loves his spirit,
he spreads such happiness

Love and smiles of goodness
makes this time the very best

'Cause everybody loves the big fat man
with the suit and the long white beard

He ain't no hippie, nossiree, why,
he ain't even weird

He's everything to everyone,
the symbol of a happy cause

Everybody loves the big fat man

That swingin' Santa Claus

SANTA

George Smith will always be Santa Claus to me. He actually went to Santa Claus School and got a degree. His Santa suits were beautiful... several over the years... and he had the most gorgeous beard and wig I believe I've ever seen. How bittersweet that he died on Christmas Eve, 1993.

George did many charitable things and sprinkled a lot of cheer. He gave of his time, from Thanksgiving until Christmas... visited every kindergarten, civic club... and he and I always did the Pancake Day at Fox Restaurant downtown; then we'd go from there out to the hospital.

I'd have toys for the children, but we would also visit the older people.

Back in those days... this sounds terrible... it's cruel, but it happened... At the hospital, they called it "dumpin' time." People would bring their old folks out there and leave 'em so they wouldn't have to fool with them during the Christmas holidays; and they could go off somewhere and celebrate.

I'd get a list so we'd know their first names and find out if they could have a stick of candy; then we'd begin making our Santa rounds.

Delightful, dainty little ol' ladies... so many of 'em, it was the last Christmas they had on earth. I went in the room first and they were in there by themselves.

"Well, hello, Cousin Tuny."

"Cuz, I'm gonna tell ya somethin'. There is a good-lookin' man outside that wants to come into your bedroom."

"Oh well... well... well... let me fix myself."
Cutest things you ever saw. Some of 'em 90, 95 years old.

George came in and said "Well, hello there, little Marilee. I remember comin' to see you when you were little-bitsy. Yes, sir, comin' and bringin' you a toy and stick candy and a little fruit."

She gazed up at George... "Oh Santa, that's right. You sure did." It was beautiful. That man spread so much happiness...

cuz

One Christmas Eve there was a terrible wreck out here on 45 South. Mother, father, a four-year-old little girl and a nineteen-month-old. The mother and the 19-month-old were killed. The father was critically injured. The little four-year-old girl was injured but not critically, minor injuries.

When they brought her out of the emergency room, I was down there... we hadn't gone up to the hospital rooms yet. What happened... they were going down to the grandparents to spend Christmas in Corinth, Mississippi, and they had all their Santa Claus and everything in the back of the car. It was all destroyed; car totalled. They said I could see the little girl before they took her upstairs. Her name was Penelope... Penny.

I said "Penny, do you know who I am?"

"Yes, you're Cousin Tuny, 'cause I see you on television when I visit my grandmother in Corinth."

And Santa came around the corner.

"Hello, Penny, ol' Santa's sorry you had a -- "

"Oh, Santa Claus, I was afraid you wouldn't know where I am."

Well, that triggered off some big stuff in my heart and mind. We went upstairs and saw the children. Then I went to McClellan's Department Store and spoke to Mr. Cook, who was the manager. I told him what had happened... this child would not have a Christmas except for the one toy that I left her.

And the guys at Smith Funeral Home -- Jack and Jerry, George's twin sons -- went out and bought her two or three things 'cause she was up there by herself. Anyway, the grandparents were on their way from Corinth. And Mr. Cook filled my trunk with toys. I remembered I had some toys in my attic that I kept, mainly for terminally ill children, having gotten them from a

126

chemical company who put me on their board-at-large... I had this beautiful doll up there...

I bet I had $300 worth of toys by the time I got to the nurses' station.

I told them "Now listen, in the morning... I didn't bring these. Santa Claus left 'em, okay?"

The Head Nurse said "Oh Tuny, I can't wait. This is wonderful."

I went into her room. "Penny?"

"Hey, Cousin Tuny."

"Penny, Santa sent me back up here to tell you to be a real good girl, do what they say, close your eyes and go to sleep, and your grandmother and grandfather will be here in a little while... and Santa's gonna tiptoe in here while you're asleep tonight and leave you some surprises."

She gave me such a warm smile.

"So good night, Penny, sleep tight."

"Cousin Tuny?"

"Yes, Little Cousin, what is it?"

"Merry Christmas."

It ripped my heart out. There was that little four-year-old, her mother dead, her little sister dead, and her father at the point of death on Christmas Eve.

But Penny had a big Christmas.

It took us a long time to get around to all the rooms; nevertheless, we just laid that time out to wish everybody a Merry Christmas. It was well worth it.

MR. COLIE / UNCLE CHARLIE

Mr. Colie Chandler was a little old man, looked like a hard knot on a log. He was the engineer on the Illinois Central Railroad that my father worked. Well, he retired -- older than St. Louis.

One morning, Aaron and I were walkin' by the Bank of Commerce downtown, on the way to get a cup of coffee. Mr. Colie was sittin' in front of the newsstand his son Eddie owned... and he was parked there all drawn up in a little hard knot in the front seat of the car.

We went over to see him.

"Hey there, Little Felix."

That's what a lot of the old men called me, 'Little Felix'... 'cause they watched me tap dancing with Daddy.

"Mr. Colie, hey to you."

Aaron said "Mr. Colie, what are you doin' with yourself nowadays?"

"Hell, ain't but two things left for me to do at my age: one of 'em is try and remember some sonofabitch's name and the other one's to try and find the men's room."

Uncle Charlie was my father's brother. Daddy was a tall six-footer, but Uncle Charlie was just like a little dried-up mouse. He lived a l-o-n-g life; he was even older than Mr. Colie.

When Uncle Charlie died, Miss Evie (the 'good'

stepmother) and I went to the funeral at Lanier Funeral Home. There were two rooms full of family and relatives; immediate family in one room and the rest of us in the next room. Where we were sitting, I could see the area in front of the casket and Uncle Charlie's nose stickin' up. And I could see Aunt Fanny, Uncle Charlie's wife, who weighed 300 pounds if she weighed an ounce... salt of the earth, dear and sweet.

William Lanier came up to Aunt Fanny and asked "Mrs. Branch, you wanna go view the remains?"

"Yessir."

She covered two chairs, she was so big. Took two men to get her up out of the seats. They walked her up to the casket.

William Lanier said "My, isn't he handsome."

Well, I got tickled because Uncle Charlie never had been accused of being handsome. He was kinda homely when he was alive, and he was just as homely dead and dead homely, looked like to me. He was cleaned up, but you know...

All of a sudden, Aunt Fanny cried "Oh, I think I'm gonna faint!!" And she grabbed ahold of the side of that casket and started goin' down — William Lanier was tryin' to keep her from fallin' on top of him 'cause there'd just be nothin' left but a greasy spot and a little piece of chin if she'd fallen on him. Took about four or five men to get her back to her seat.

During the funeral, this country preacher got wound up and, man, I thought he was never gonna shut up. There was some idiot cousin from up in Henderson County somewhere wearin' thongs, and she came clunkin' across in front of me, to the rest room which was right there close to us. Right in the middle of the thing, got up and went, shut the door — she sounded like a cow on a flat rock; flushed the commode... it reverberated throughout the entire funeral home. I thought, well, I'm gonna have to get up and leave here myself... just leave the whole thing...

I started thinkin' about when Uncle Charlie was gonna paint the outside of our house... Mother got so mad at him she ran him off; that little woman got up on that ladder and painted the house herself. Uncle Charlie went over to the fillin' station that was across the highway from where we lived and he bought a can of Vienna sausages and some crackers. Mother would never allow me to have anything like that.

I was standin' there and he said "Would you like to have some of this, Doris?"

"Well, yessir, I never have had any."

So the old fool didn't give me any Vienna sausage... you know the jelly stuff around the sausage... he put that on a cracker and said "That's the best part, I'm givin' you the best part."

And I just stood there and ate it — didn't know any better. I thought it was wonderful.

Uncle Charlie was a dude.

JUST CUZ - BEIN' TUNY

Another memorable Thursday night... I was paged... "Cousin Tuny, you're needed over at third floor." So I went to the nurses' station.

At that time, the Sheriff of Madison County was Cecil Burlison. Cecil's grandfather was in the hospital having cataract surgery. In those days, when you had cataract surgery, you had to lie on your back, real still for so many hours; and they put little pie plates on their eyes for bandages.

The grandfather, who was in his 90's and little-bitty, had heard me on TV that afternoon saying that I was going to the hospital that night to visit the children.

Cecil said "Grandpa is about to have a fit to see you."

"Okay, take me in there to see him."

All stretched out, looked like he was about 5'4" at the most lying there. They had the railings up on each side of the hospital bed. Tons of people in the room... and he's running his mouth off somethin' fierce.

I walked up to the bed and said "Hey, Cuz."

"Is that you, Cousin Tuny?"... He had the little pie plate things on his eyes.

I said "Yes."

I reached out and took his hand -- he grabbed hold of me -- jerked me over into the bed with him, over those big ol' rails. And there I was in bed with that little old man...

I mean, he was all over me!

"Lord, I've always wanted to get in the bed with you, Cousin Tuny."

Everybody in the room was screaming with laughter, and there I was tryin' to get out of bed with this little guy. Somebody told the nurses, so they showed up too.

I'm glad he didn't have a feather pillow... I was in enough mess as it was.

But I finally got out. And I said "You may think he's 90-something, but he's acting much younger than that. There's still a lot of fire in that furnace, folks."

That little feller was tough!

They teased me about that for a long time. But I'm tellin' ya, my stomach was sore; in fact, I was sore all over for some time from being pulled over those bed railings.

It was quite a situation, one in which Mother Nature and Father Time failed me again.

OFF THE AIR & INTO THE FRAY

WDXI-TV was sold and, in 1967, I left television. They sold WDXI Radio in 1973 — I left in '75. The new owners had used batteries for brains and no heart whatsoever. So I left and went to WJAK. They hauled off and sold WJAK Radio in a couple of years. I left WJAK — I'd been free-lancing all along, doing marketing and public relations for Old Hickory Mall — then I went into the Mall as Manager and Marketing Director in 1980. Be damned if they didn't sell Old Hickory Mall in 1985, which put me literally into General Hospital, as Marketing and Public Relations Director. So I've had four businesses sold out from under me. Now if they sell the hospital, I won't mind, since I've retired to follow other adventures.

At WJAK the movie theatres were my accounts. They were bringing in fifteen thousand dollars a year, twenty percent of which was my commission.

The station refused to advertise a movie ... it was about teenagers going off to camp, going to have sex, but didn't... anyway, I went to see the film and it had an outstanding moral in it...

The theatres cancelled their advertising, wouldn't ever run again, and I don't blame 'em.

They were trying to get rid of me because they thought I made too much money that year, working strictly on commission.

They pronounced, "You know, after all, Tuny, you're 55."

"Yeah, and, I can work circles around anybody's butt anytime and anyday, and don't you ever forget it."

cuz

"Well, you do have a lot of energy. But, after all, you're a woman."

I looked around and replied, "So write God a dirty note. "

As my momma used to say, they'll get their comeuppance.

I wonder if women will ever get the recognition they deserve...

WOMAN OF THE YEAR

She's excited, delighted
She's glad, she's sad
She's being honored tonight
With the best to be had
She's been chosen to be
The queen of them all
She's humble, she's grateful
And she feels ten feet tall

She's smiling
And yet through that smile
There's a tear
As the time for unveiling
Draws very near
She's someone we all know
Star of Altrusa's show
She's the Woman of the Year

cuz

I was Jackson-Madison County Woman of the Year in 1963; and wrote the above song the night of the Altrusa Club dinner. It was held in the Gold Room of the New Southern Hotel. Gee, I really miss that beautiful room. The New Southern is still there, it was an old folks' home; pre-tornado - 2003, but I believe it will always be there.

I told the children a story to get them dressed in their best bib-and-tucker. When we got to Ruth's to pick her up, I told them that I was Woman of the Year. And they had to wait in the kitchen at the New Southern before the announcement. My nephew Sonny played piano that night; he didn't know about it either, and he escorted me up to the table.

The thing about being Woman of the Year that touched me more than anything was the fact that the nurses in the pediatric wing at General Hospital wrote a beautiful nomination for me. They went around and got the parents of the sick children to sign the nomination. That meant more to me than getting it. That's what it's all about.

cuz

American Heart Association
Congressman "Fats" Everett, Tuny, Jack Fritts,
and Judge Walter Baker Harris

CUZ

The Charlie Baker Band

Tuny's TV Crew Cousins

The Cisco Kid, Tuny, and Blackjack

The Author and Co-Author of "CUZ"

Tuny and Jayne Mansfield

We request the honor of your viewing

"THE COUSIN TUNY SHOW"
Christmas Day, at 5 p.m.
on W D X I - T V

For Our Annual Christmas Show
So We Can Especially Wish You
A MERRY CHRISTMAS!

Thank You,
Pat, Cindy, Jimmy, and Connie Freeman

P. S. Oh, yes, Our Mother will be there too!
It's her show — you see, she's **Cousin Tuny!**

CUZ

"COUSIN TUNY"

You are invited to appear on THE COUSIN TUNY SHOW with
me on _____ Be at the
WDXI-TV Studio in the Williams Building in Jackson
not later than 3:30 P.M. on this date. PLEASE LET ME
KNOW IF YOU CAN OR CANNOT BE HERE. Bring this card
with you. I am looking forward to seeing you.
                     Best wishes,

Window at Holland and Gilliam

Doris, her children, "Woman of the Year" 1963

CUZ

Carl Perkins and Tuny

My Soulmate   Me   My Soul Brother

Greg, Carl, Stan - Perkins

Tuny, Naomi Judd, Carl, and Wynonna Judd

cuz

"Big J leads the way!"
Cheering on baseball in Jackson, Tennessee

Tuny takes a break -
Clowning around

Tuny's children and grandchildren

Tuny and Great Grandson, Jack Little

Reaction from Telethon's success!

HORSES AND ME

Never ridden a horse in my life...

The Cotillion Club had their first annual horse show and all the proceeds were going to the Cerebral Palsy Center. They asked me if I would ride in the Celebrity Class. 'Way they talked, somebody would put me on a horse and they'd just kinda lead me around the ring... Well, it was me and Matt Kisber, the State Representative and the State Senator and Super Wolfe, who ran a radio station.

They put me up on this black horse. His name was Lucky and he belonged to a 14-year-old girl who lived on the other side of Humboldt. There I was with my pantaloons on, sittin' up there... and I got to talkin' to the horse; I thought, well, I've gotta make friends with this dude.

When they called the Celebrity Class, the little girl started leadin' me, tellin' me what to do.

"This is Lucky's first horse show, too."

I thought, well, this is just bully-bully, hoop-de-do. She leads me into the ring and, all of a sudden, she hits that horse on his left back flank — and a-way he goes — takes off with me on him. I thought, oh my God, I'm gonna get killed right here in front of all these people — tremendous crowd.

The horse thought he was entering the Chase Manhattan Bank, I think, and he had not made a deposit in two weeks — he started makin' droppings all the way around the ring.

As I passed the crowd, I said "You know, I have a great

effect on animals. Um-hm. At least everything's coming out all right."

We had to stop the horses in front of the main portion of the crowd. And the ringmaster said "Please reverse your horse."

I stared back at him... "I don't even see a prundle here... there's no gearshift."

I was on the horse for about 15 minutes and I won the Blue Ribbon, First Place. I gave the girl the ribbon and said "This is your first Blue Ribbon and, wherever you decide to hang it, remember that the horse really won this himself."

Then I had to ride the horse by myself in the Winner's Ring.

As I passed the crowd, I said "Look, y'all, I'm a little old lady, I'm not supposed to be doin' this"... just trottin' along.

When I left the ring, they said "You can get down now." 'Oh, really?...!'

"I'm glued to this horse."

They had to lift me off that thing, and when I went to the ground I went aaallll the way down.

"Man, the legs done gone to sleep here, folks."
Anyway, we raised some money for the Cerebral Palsy Center, and that's what I really cared about. I had some parts sore I didn't know I owned; nonetheless, it was worth it.

By the way, the next year I rode a stick horse...

Never emceed a horse show in my life...

Cecil and Lillian Parris, in Savannah at the Kadets of America Headquarters, had me out there for the show.

cuz

I always had fun working there because we were such good friends, too. Cecil gave me little Kadet rifles for years to take to the children. Ruth would drive with me to Savannah — we'd load the trunk with toy rifles and — clippity-clop — back to Jackson. For many moons I was runnin' guns to the hospital. The kids loved 'em.

Cecil was a wonderful person. Everybody called him "Catfish" Parris because he started the Catfish Derby. Tennessee River catfish and hush puppies... mmmm... delish. My daughter Cindie used to sing and appear with me; she was Sweetheart of the Kadets of America as an adolescent and sang to the young Kadets at various events.

They brought in all these fine-looking horses, and I was standing there and heard "Now the mare with fold"...

I thought, What in the world is a mare with a fold, is that an accordion-pleated somethin'? That was 'mare with colt.' I didn't know what I was talkin' about.

They had a big parade for the Catfish Derby, a festive annual celebration in those parts...

I was asked to ride one of those miniature rocking horses, like from a merry-go-round... they were on springs and you rock back and forth on 'em...

They took one of those cotton-pickin' things and put it on a platform, and I threw candy out. One of the Kadets pulled me — the saddle of that horse and my saddle didn't fit — it was for a little child, not my south end. He pulled me down the middle of the street in Savannah.   When I got off that thing, I was raw... had to see a doctor before I could go onstage that night as emcee at the auditorium for the Derby...

I mean, that young Kadet would pull, then he'd stop, then he'd pull, then he'd stop... and that little rocky horse would buck back-and-forth, back-and-forth, back-and-forth through the whole parade.

I've ridden about everything in parades... floats, ponies, elephants, Brahma bulls... but the little rocky horse wins the ribbon for the roughest ride — so far.

I'm here to say that's the extent of my horse-ridin'.

DOGS AND ME

Never been ridden by a dog in my life...

The Greenfield Manufacturing Company in Greenfield, Tennessee was owned and run by the Prinze family. They manufactured jackets, coats, etc., for Sears Roebuck.

They beckoned me up there one night to emcee a fashion show, in my pantaloons, for a back-to-school to-do, and the wheels were gonna be there from Sears and all that jazz. They invited Ruth and me to dinner first.

That day I had been in Huntington, Tennessee riding in the Carroll County Fair Parade. I was on a float with Mrs. Mary Sue Jolly's Kindergarten. We got out to the fairground, I got down off the float and walked through the fairground, giving autographs and visiting with the good people. Then I had to get in the car and drive home. I got here just in time to do my TV show; and when I signed off the air, I didn't have time to change clothes, had the same pantaloons on... just kinda patched my makeup and hurried so we wouldn't be late for the dinner in Greenfield...

The Prinzes had a beautiful home. Ruth and I walked in and went back into the family room to have a glass of wine.

Here came this little black poodle... his name was Louis the XIV. I was sittin' on the couch and that little poodle jumped up, started lickin' me and hasslin' — I mean he was goin' into a real sex heat stroke there. They finally got so embarrassed, they took him out.

We finished our wine and went into the big dining room. Frank and Dixie Prinze had two little girls; one was eleven and one was twelve years old at that time. I was seated next to the girls on one side of the table, and Ruth was directly across the table in front of me...

Ruth dropped her napkin, it slid off her lap onto the floor. She reached down to get it, just as I felt somethin' grab ahold of my leg. I lifted the tablecloth up a bit and that little dog had gotten back in and was making love to my leg. I mean, he was humping like there was no tomorrow.

Ruth saw that, glanced at me under the table, right slick lookin'... I got hysterical and I couldn't get the dog off my leg; I couldn't say anything because those two little girls were seated at the table. Then they got up and excused themselves 'cause they were going somewhere else.

Finally, I turned around and said "Frank, this dog is makin' love to my leg." He had to pull that dog off me.

We figured later... evidently, in the fairgrounds in Huntington, there had to be some animals there that were in season, in heat, and somehow that dog picked up on their scent since I had been around them... it sent that little fella crazy.

From then on, when I got a letter from Frank, he said "P.S. Louie sends his love."

FEMALE CHAUVINIST PIGS

Never met a pig I didn't like...

I was speaking to one of the "clubs"... little old ladies with their Ways and Means Committee... the old business and the new business... big-time stuff. I really let loose on 'em... and I get so tickled 'cause these little old women are somethin'.

I told 'em a joke about the couple who bought the pig farm; they never had done any pig farming before. They had these pigs... months went by and they didn't see any other pigs and couldn't understand why. So the husband went down to the country store and said "I wanna ask y'all somethin'. What about these pigs?"

They said "You need to get the vet to come out there an' look at 'em."

The vet went out and said "No wonder you don't have any little pigs... these are female pigs... you gotta have a boar. Farmer Brown lives up the road here, he's got a whole herd of boars. You take the pigs up there and get 'em all serviced up."

The next mornin' the young farmer hauled all the pigs up in the back of his pickup truck, kept 'em at Farmer Brown's all day and brought 'em back.

He asked the vet "How will I know if it took?"
"If they're standing on the high ground, it didn't take. If they're wallering in the mud, it took."

The next mornin', after he'd had 'em at Farmer Brown's all day the day before, he told his wife "Look out there and see."

She said "They're on the high ground."

"Okay."

So he hauled 'em back up in the truck again, carried 'em to Farmer Brown's a second time. Brought 'em back.

The next mornin', looks. They're on the high ground. They're not wallerin' in the mud. Didn't take. He took 'em the third time.

"Oh Lord, maybe, maybe."

Next mornin'. Little wife looks out. "Well, they're not on the high ground."

"Then they're wallerin' in the mud? It took?"

She said "Naw, they're not wallerin' in the mud."

"Where are they?"

"They're all up in the truck."

And these little women went "Oh... oh me... ah, ah, oh..."

Those people, when they get excited like that... they try to act like it shocks 'em, but they like it. They're the kind, when they leave the city limits goin' somewhere, they go wild.

JUST CUZ - BEIN' TUNY

I was talking to a family in the hospital who had someone in Intensive Care. This great big fat gal walked up — she must have weighed 250 pounds — at least a head taller than me — built like Dolly Parton, but just big fat everywhere. And right from the sticks.

She tapped me on the shoulder... "'Scuse me, but ain't you Cuddin Tuny?"

"I'm afraid so."

She turned around and said "Momma, I told you thatus her. I told you. When I heard her speak, I knowed it was her... Lord, Tuny, I never thought I'd get to see you live and in person!" [Huh?] "I used to watch you on the TV every evenin'. I'd get off the school bus and go lickety-split right up there to the house. I always did wanna hug your neck."

"Well, just help yourself."

She grabbed me and my face went in between the big boobs into the valley. And she didn't turn loose. I thought I was going to smother to death. I was hyperventilating... got right dizzy. That ol' gal put the death grip on me! I thought, holy mackerel, she's gonna literally love me to death here. It was a large show for passersby.

"Lord, I didn't mean to squeeze ya so hard, but I just wanted to hug ya; just to think I seen Cuddin Tuny — live and in person!!"

JIM RAY

Mr. Jim Ray came to Jackson as manager of Sears Roebuck in Old Hickory Mall. That was my account; and I was heavily involved with marketing and the Merchants Association when the Mall opened in 1967. Since Sears was one of the anchor stores and he was very active in the Merchants Association, I worked with Jim a good bit. He was an extremely nice man. We helped each other; had a marvelous working relationship.

I was sitting in his office when he had just found out that he had leukemia. I had my billfold open, showing him pictures of my children, and the change part came open. I have a little cross that I carry and it fell out.

This cross was given to me aboard a plane... I was sitting next to Ida Nicks. She was Governor Frank Clement's aunt, and Ida and me were real good buddies. I saw that little aluminum cross hangin' from a bracelet and I said "Where'd you get that?"

She said "You mean you don't have a cross for your pocket?"

"No."

"I wanna be the one to give you one."

I still have it and I cherish it.

When Jim saw it he said "Oh, Tuny, where did you get that cross?" And I told him.

I said "You don't have a cross for your pocket?"
"No."

"Well, allow me..."

CUZ

I had some that I had ordered and gave him one.
"Oh, thank you, Tuny. This means so much to me."
"You just grab ahold of that cross and hang on, Cuz."

And I gave him the poem that went with it, written by Verna Thomas of McGehee, Arkansas:

> I carry a cross in my pocket,
>
> A simple reminder to me
>
> Of the fact that I am a Christian,
>
> No matter where I may be.
>
> This little cross is not magic,
>
> Nor is it a good-luck charm:
>
> It isn't meant to protect me
>
> From any physical harm.
>
> It is not for identification,
>
> For all the world to see...
>
> It's simply an understanding
>
> Between my Saviour and me.
>
> When I put my hand in my pocket
>
> To bring out a coin or a key,
>
> The cross is there to remind me
>
> Of all that He's done for me.

It reminds me, too, to be thankful
For my blessings, day by day;
And to strive to serve Him better
In all that I do or say.

It is also a daily reminder
Of the peace and comfort I share
With all who know my Master,
And give themselves to His care.

So I carry a cross in my pocket
Reminding me, no one but me,
That Jesus Christ is Lord of my life
If only I'll let Him be.

The next week he called me. "Tuny, you comin' out to the Mall?"

"Yes."

"I'd like to see you."

When I walked in, he said "Do you mind if I get some of those crosses and give 'em away?"

"That's what it's all about, Cuz."

"I went to see Dr. Shaw in Memphis. I reached in my

pocket to get a list of questions I wanted to ask him; when I pulled out the list, in my hand was that cross. He asked me where I got it, and I told him. He said 'Oh, I would love to have some to give to my staff and the physicians on my staff.'"

I said "You must have a super-nice doctor."

From then on, as long as this man lived, he gave out crosses. He would call me ever' so often and say "Tuny, I'm just havin' more fun."

On Christmas Eve I had laryngitis, which was not unusual for me when I was workin' 16, 18 hours a day that time of year. That morning I was in Fox Restaurant at Pancake Day. They came and got me, took me out to Sears. It was before the store opened and they were havin' a party for Jim because he was forced to retire. They knew that his time was very short.

I sang to him in a whispered voice, because I was about to lose it all...

MR. SEARS AND ROEBUCK

Dear Mr. Sears and Roebuck

I've been sittin' here a-thumbin' thru your book

Page 199 shows a stove that's mighty fine

And a feller in an apron like a cook

Oh, Mr. Sears and Roebuck

That electric stove's away above my class

Now, it's a beauty, yes, indeed

But the thing I really need

Is that guy to teach me how to cook with gas.

I don't want the stove, it's the kind I'd like to buy

But I ain't makin' much singin' ballads

You can keep the stove, but if I could have that guy

He could — toss me around like his salads

Oh, Mr. Sears and Roebuck

I've been checkin' your supplies for tennis courts

Now, there is something I should get,

Not a racket or a net

But I sure could use that rascal in the shorts.

Oh, Mr. Sears and Roebuck

Your canoe on page 343

Well, it's the type that I would pick

But I'm up a diff'rent crick

Can't you send a feller here to paddle me?

I don't want a bath, soapy water makes me howl

Don't the folks in your ads ever mind it?

You can keep your bath, you can keep

your turkish towel

Only — send me the sheik from behind it.

CUZ

Don't mean to fuss, Oh, Roebuck,

But you'll never fill my order, it appears

Now, if your shortage is acute

I'm an easy girl to suit

I'll shut up if you will send me Mr. Sears

(if he ain't taken)

I'll shut up if you will send me Mr. Sears...

That night Jim Ray sent me a beautiful book — "Leaves of Gold" — that he inscribed. I wouldn't take anything for it.

We were sitting down for dinner when the phone rang and Connie answered it; I couldn't speak above a whisper.

"Mother, Mr. Jim Ray wants to talk to you."

I took the phone and said "Hey, Cuz."

"I know that you have laryngitis and you came out this morning anyway, as sick as you were. Tuny, I just wanted to tell you... This is my last Christmas on earth. I want you to know how much I love you, how much you have meant to me and my family, and I want to wish you a Merry, Merry Christmas."

He died in January. I went to his funeral at First Presbyterian Church; and, as I was sitting there, the minister said "The greatest joy Jim Ray had the last months of his life was giving a cross to everybody who came to see him, a cross for their pocket."

GOLD MEDAL / CAMP BLUEBIRD

Every year the hospital administrative staff and department heads go on a retreat. We usually went to Holiday Inn Conference Center in Olive Branch, Mississippi. They have this magnificent hotel down there with golf course and the whole nine yards. And this is where they train their management. Big industries also go there for training... they have an amphitheatre where you can have speakers, any audio-visual equipment you might need, etc.

The Holiday Inn invited us to a lovely reception for Kennedy McKinney, the young black man who was the Olympic Gold Medal winner in Featherweight Boxing. He's from this little town, Olive Branch, which is not too far out of Memphis. He said he didn't wanna have anything in Memphis; preferred to come back to Olive Branch, Mississippi.

Looked like the whole town turned out in the amphitheatre as Kennedy, in a white tux, shook hands with everybody. There were telegrams from the Governor and the Mayor... many congratulatory remarks.

Kennedy's mother was the custodian at the elementary school there in Olive Branch. He called her to the stage, took his Gold Medal out of a box, put it around her neck and kissed her.

I thought that was a real sweet thing. Not many dry eyes in the audience.

I found it amusing when he presented his siblings, a whole bunch of them.

"Those were my brothers and sisters on my mother's side.

CUZ

Now I want to introduce my brothers and sisters on my father's side."

I looked around and thought, uh, um-hm, okay.

General Hospital and Tennessee Telephone Pioneers co-sponsored what we call Camp Bluebird at Lakeshore in Eva, Tennessee. It's a beautiful Methodist camp on the river for cancer patients and their counselors.

I was asked to be a counselor and to do a show for them. It isn't a sad time; on the contrary, it's fun, a happy time. Down on the riverbank there are built-in concrete bleachers with a big wooden Cross that looms up above. Breathtaking. You feel so close to the Almighty, with nothing but nature surrounding you. That's where we would gather for Devotional. And if anyone wished to say anything, they would.

To see these people stand up and say "I didn't really know how to appreciate life or to live life until I was diagnosed. And I want to thank everybody for this experience, to be together."

This happens twice a year, in October and in May. So many go back every year because it's a party time. It's a time for crafts; and they build birdhouses for bluebirds; they always put on a show... the food is fantastic. Good fellowship.

It makes you sit up and take notice. I sat there lookin' at all those people thinking, Geemanee, am I gonna be the next one to be diagnosed with cancer? It's rampant. What a good feeling if you can help ease and bring a little happiness to somebody who has it.

Excerpt from "God's Chosen Few" The Camp Bluebird Story:

PRAYER FROM CAMP BLUEBIRD

Dear Lord,

Thank You for another day,

Within this life of mine.

Let me live it well,

Whatever I may find.

Bestow from Thy abundance,

Whatever I may lack,

To use the hours wisely,

For I cannot have them back.

Lord, thank You for another day,

In which to make amends,

For the little slights or petty words,

Inflicted on my friends.

For sometimes losing patience,

With problems that I find.

Lord, thank You for another chance,

To show Your Love in kind.

For yesterday is over,

And tomorrow's far away,

And I remain committed,

To the good I do today.

I wake up every morning... gratefully.

cuz

NORTH AND SOUTH

A good many years ago I had throat surgery; then I began having difficulty swallowing, and thought, hmm, better go check this out. So I went back to see Dr. Swan Burrus, Jr.

He mashed on the throat and he mashed on the throat... he said "Tuny, there's nothing wrong with your throat; but while you're here, I wanna give you a complete physical. Your throat's okay, that's just a little stress." Stress... that's a word I think they've ruptured, overused. I suspect a lot of people use that as a crutch.

The good doctor did the pelvic and said "You've got to have a hysterectomy, Tuny."

"Oh, come on, I've been through menopause."

"I won't remove the ovaries."

"For God sakes, let the dead rest in peace there... no, don't take them. They've been overworked and underpaid."

"I'm going to take out your uterus and tie up your bladder."

"Oh, take out the baby buggy and leave the playpen."

He did take a tuck in the bladder.

I told him "Hell, you don't know the north from the south, do you?"

Story of my life... I go to the doctor to see about my throat and end up... the north end's fine, the south end's gotta go.

A few years ago... tuck city, part two... I had four incisions, two up inside and two opposite each other on the lower abdomen, and in between those two incisions on my abdomen there was a tube that went all the way through to my bladder, and that tube was attached to a tube that went into a bag that hung down —

I told 'em I knew I was the bag lady, I didn't know I was gonna carry it around on my leg... I've seen these little old people with their little sacks... I thought, Gee, I feel right at home now.

It'd been the third or fourth day post-surgery, and two of the nurses came in. They had rubber gloves, and said they were gonna teach me to do something.

"The doctor would like to remove this tube from your abdomen before you go home from the hospital. If not, if you can't handle this, you'll have to carry the bag home. Then he'll have to take the tube out when you go back to see him, or when your bladder starts performing as it should." I said "What are you gonna do?"

They put on the rubber gloves, rolled up my bed, and put a magnifying mirror down in between my legs. "We're gonna teach you to catheterize yourself."

"Say what?"

They brought out this little catheter thing. I looked in the mirror. "My God! That's the ugliest thing I've ever seen in my life. And the older it gets, the uglier it gets. Look, my momma always told me that if I fooled around with myself, that I would go deaf, dumb and blind. And I still believe that. Now she didn't say nobody else couldn't fool around down there, but she said I couldn't."

When they stopped laughing, the nurses showed me where to put the thing... And about the time I was gonna hit pay dirt, my bladder went into the damndest spasm, I thought I was going to faint I was in such pain.

I said "I don't know what this is, but y'all, I can't get my breath."

They called the doctor and gave me a shot. Needless to say, I brought the bag home with me and measured myself and da-da-da-da... The next week, when the doctor took the tube out, my bladder went into another spasm — I saw stars, passed Mars, Venus and everybody!...

When I see the nurses from that floor, they tell me "Tuny, every time we go in to try to teach a woman to catheterize herself, we get to tellin' 'em what you did and said... you'd be surprised how many women it's relaxed so they can do it."

"Well, I ain't pokin' no kind o' stuff in there, not this old girl, uh-uh, noooooo, baby, uh-uh." I was afraid I'd injure myself. That's awful.

Now I just hope I don't mess up the washer I got in my faucet.

When I went back for a checkup, my young surgeon, Dr. Yarbro, said "Don't lift anything heavy, drink lots of liquids, and you're doing real well. Do you want to ask me anything?"

"Yes, I do. What if some good-lookin' man propositions me? What should I tell him?"

"Tell him to be gentle."

I gazed at him... "Look, I'm the funny man, you're the straight man, got it?"

He turned so red in the face... a cutie-pie when he was a little boy on my TV show, and still a cutie-pie.

BEGIN THE BIDET

My first encounter with a bidet was in Johnson City, Tennessee. I was Heart Sunday Chairman for the state and flew all over to entertain for the Heart Association. I was to speak and sing at East Tennessee State University. They had a reception/cocktail party first, in a beautiful home... heart specialists, politicians, etc.

When it came time for us to go, the lady of the house carried me back to her lovely bathroom so I could change into my pantaloons and Tuny makeup. And I thought I had better participate, not knowing how accessible a powder room would be later.

So I transformed into Tuny. I sat down on the commode, my foot went back and, all of a sudden, this warm water came up from somewhere in the commode and hit me right between my Democrat and my Republican.

I came up off that thing, turned around and thought, Well, I didn't know I was so strong that it's hittin' me back!

When I went out, I told the woman, "I had an unexpected meeting with your — "

She said "Oh, I meant to tell you that there was a bidet in there."

"Didn't you hear me holler 'Somebody kiss me'!?"

CODE PENAL

Dolores Moore, Vice-President of Nursing, called me. "Tuny, I want you to have lunch with me and Dr. Lane Bicknell, the urologist. He has a project he wants to talk to you about."

And we set the date. The day came for the lunch meeting and Dolores was too busy to go. "You go ahead, you can handle it." I said okay.

I met Dr. Bicknell and his nurse at The Hut. We sat down and I said "Now, Dr. Bicknell, what can I do for you?"

"I want you to do some marketing on impotence. We're gonna have a seminar here, and I want to get the word out the best way possible."

"Alright, fine. Tell me about this."

"A lot of men with prostate problems have penal implants."

I said "Uh-huh... how does that work?"

He gets these paper napkins and starts drawin' little pictures of all these little penises and all these little things that they put in 'em.

And he said "Now there's the pump"...

I thought, I could see some man makin' mad love and say, wait a minute, my pump ain't workin' just right.

"And then there are shots men can take to become potent for so many hours."

"Dr. Bicknell, if I could get half a pint of that stuff, I

could make a fortune on Court Square, 'cause those old guys up there, just one more time, they'd give us everything they had for the rest of their lives."

We laughed about it, but we also managed to bring in a very good crowd for the seminar, since it does affect so many men.

I couldn't help it. All I could think of was a jingle... When you're down and out, Hold up your head and shout, Give me an implant today... Up, up and away...

TUCKUS

Dave Richman's daughter Elaine had her bas mitzvah at the Jewish temple, and I was one of the few gentiles invited. After the ceremony we went downstairs for wine and all that good Jewish food.

I asked Dave "You've got to tell me some words to say"...

"Mazeltov means Congratulations and Good Shabbas is Happy Sabbath."

I go "Mazeltov, Good Shabbas, Mazeltov, Good Shabbas"...

Dave's brother Sammy, from Memphis, was standing in a corner — he's a sight.

He motioned to me "Come over here, Tuny."

"Hey, Cuz, Mazeltov and Good Shabbas."

He said "Mazeltov to you. We're so impressed that you want to be a part of this and get into the jargon. Now if anybody asks you how you learn all this, tell 'em you keep it all up here in your tuckus," pointing to his head.

I said "Oh, thanks a lot."

I go clippin' over to this whole group of Jewish cousins... "Mazeltov and Good Shabbas. See, I'm doin' so good."

One of them said "How'd you learn that?"

I stuck my finger up on my head... "Keep it all up here in my tuckus."

Cut to the chase. [When in doubt, exit laughing]

With all my south end trouble, you'd think I woulda known automatically where my tuckus was.

cuz

JUST CUZ - BEIN' TUNY

I was walking through the hospital and saw three or four people standing by the elevator who I knew.

I said "Do you have somebody here?"

"Just friends."

I gave 'em my card... "If I can do anything, let me know."

Somebody tapped me on the shoulder; I turned around to see a middle-aged woman.

"Excuse me, I hate to do this. But are you really Cousin Tuny?"

"Yes, ma'am."

"Lord have mercy. Momma, Momma, Momma, get over here, right quick... come on over here, Momma, hurry now!"

Here came this little old lady that'd been through Medicare twice. Her hair was snow-white, had a little bun on her head, carryin' her pocketbook in the front with both hands holdin' the handles... sweet.

She said "How's that?"

"Momma, look here, you know who this is?"

"No."

The daughter touched me on the shoulder and said "Say somethin' to Momma."

"Well, Cuz, it's good to see you."

"Lord God, it's Cousin Tuny. Honey, I declare, I see you on the TV with them little children all the time. Do you know you sound just like yourself?"

I said "Thank you very much."

I hadn't been on television for 20 years at that point, but I'm sure she was talkin' about the children's telethons that I co-emceed with Carl Perkins, I say to myself in consolation.

As I walked back to my office, I got to thinkin'... I sound just like myself... who else would I sound like?

There's nothin' like bein' Tuny.

SAM SIEGEL

Minnie Pearl was due to speak in Somerville on behalf of the Heart Association. She had laryngitis, so she had them call and ask me to go in her place. The Association had asked me to speak and entertain before and, with my sister Agnes' problem... a diabetic with a congestive heart... naturally, I was interested.

I was doing the television show, in the early 60's, when Bob Allen was Executive Director of the newly formed West Tennessee Heart Association, which I helped charter. Bob called and said they were gonna have a fund-raiser in Bruceton, Tennessee at the movie theatre there. All the proceeds were going to the Heart Association. I would appear onstage before the movie started with my uke and sing a few songs.

It was a little ol' country movie house... quaint. Ruth and I headed for Bruceton that night in, wouldn't you know it... pouring down rain.

I went onstage... the place was packed. No standing room. I sang some songs and I wrote a song for the Heart Association, with which I always ended my appearances.

I would sing this song when we'd go to basketball games... I'd make three or four basketball games in a night, all through the month of February. Bob Allen would call ahead and they'd stop the game when I arrived. They'd pull this great big bedsheet out in the middle of the basketball court and the cheerleaders would hold it. I'd sing my song and ask everybody to throw their change into that bedsheet for the Heart Association. We raised a ton o' money that way.

<u>H</u> means that we're here tonight

We've joined up in a band

<u>E</u> means everybody will do the best they can

<u>A</u> means over all the world

We'll spread our love and more

<u>R</u> means we will rap, rap, rap

On each and every door

<u>T</u> means that together we will work so hard

And then

We'll work and try and try and work

And then we'll try again

We'll all join hands, stand straight and tall

A winner we will be

Because we're loyal members of h-e-a-r-t

In Bruceton that night, I did about 15 minutes onstage. When I finished, this short, baldheaded man walked out with a dozen American Beauty red roses and laid 'em in my arms. He spoke with a heavy accent.

"Cousin Tuny, my name is Sam Siegel. Welcome to Bruceton. You are going to my house for dinner now."
"Well, thank you, Mr. Siegel."

I thanked the crowd, left, and Ruth and I continued on to the Siegel home. We were graciously welcomed by Gladys,

Sam's wife, and their four children. There were a whole bunch of other people there for dinner, too.

I was rather amazed when Sam cornered me... "I've learned all about you, Cousin Tuny. You are a wonderful lady."

This man was from Germany. Hitler killed his parents and some other relatives. He was one of the last Jews to get out of Germany alive during World War II. His brother Henry came over to America before Sam did, and started HIS Sportswear. Today they make Chic jeans, among many other high-quality clothes.

There's a big plant in Bruceton, which Sam toured me through. From then on, Sam and Gladys Siegel were dear, dear friends.

One evening he invited my children up for dinner and took us to the plant. We came home with about six hundred dollars worth of jackets and coats. My son Jim had every color blazer that HIS Sportswear made. What a blessing.

When Sam died of a heart attack, the city erected a statue to him in the Bruceton Square because of all the good things he did for human beings. He could not do enough for his fellowman.

When the big tornadoes hit, before the wind died down any, he had trucks leaving with clothes to take to victims. And when Agnes died, he called me and gave a substantial donation to the Heart Association in her memory... he had never met the woman but had heard me talk about her at Heart appearances.

This man was a very grateful and humbled man for what had happened to him and his success, and he shared it with people.

He had several plants in West Tennessee. One time they tried to unionize the one in Bruceton. The employees stood shoulder-to-shoulder all the way around the plant and the union never got in. He was so good to all of his workers and they appreciated it.

My friend Bill Harris did a lot of architectural work for him and drew the plans to enlarge his house. I would see Bill and his wife Charlotte there — Sam loved to have dinners and parties. He could have a seated dinner for 200 people. It was just lovely.

When Howard, the oldest child, bar mitzvahed, Ruth and I were invited to sit at the table with the family on Friday night... a very high honor. They had it at The Temple in Nashville. I have never seen such a lush, plush thing; and I've never seen such fine parties in my life.

Sam had rented the entire Holiday Inn for the weekend. The seats in The Temple were so comfortable, you just sunk down in 'em. And I was so moved by the beauty of the ceremony. Everybody was there... former Governor Gordon Browning and all the high moguls... because it was Sam Siegel's son. He was a powerful man but with as much humility as he had power.

At that time, I had different colors on either side of my hair... small wisps of red, blue, green and gold. When I went through the receiving line, Sam said to Rabbi Faulk: "Rabbi, this is Cousin Tuny, the girl with the multicolored hair."

I said "Rabbi, I'm gonna have a meeting with the Methodist Bishop because I like this Good Shabbas that you'all have in this ceremony... when you say Good Shabbas, everybody kisses everybody, and this good-lookin' man grabbed me and kissed me... and I wanna get Good Shabbas in the Methodist ritual."

The Rabbi looked at me and just died laughing. "Well, I want to hear what the Bishop says when you talk to him."

"I'll let you know."

I told the Methodist Bishop what I had done. He glanced at me and said "Aaa-ha... that's... ah... funny."

We had a lot of Heart meetings and I was with Sam and Gladys quite a bit. My life was enhanced for having known them. Sam was just a real genuine person and did a lot to make this a brighter world in which to live.

ODE TO GERTRUDE

During many of the years I broadcast the Miss Tennessee Pageant and went to Atlantic City, Gertrude Kisber was by my side. I sold her, not an easy task, on the idea of sponsoring the broadcasts; hence, she became an integral part of the Tennessee entourage... Gertrude had an impeccable sense of fashion. She had worked with her husband, Jonas, at Kisber's, known for their high quality, tasteful clothes; and took over ownership after his death. She traveled from New York to L.A. to China, all over the world, buying and keeping in touch with the latest in haute couture. She continued her fast-paced profession well into her 80's... an amazing woman.

I was already on the air one night during the Miss Tennessee competition when Gertrude came in, having been to a cocktail party. She sat down, looked up at the ramp and said "My God, look at the big a— " I smash-cut/flipped my head to Tom Britt, at that time engineer for WDXI Radio — we had a hot mike " —ass on that girl!" Tom managed to get his hand over the mike just before she said the word 'ass.'

One of the contestants came out in swimsuit and she had the boobs... made Dolly Parton look like fried eggs with broken yellows. Gertrude's eyes widened and she declared "Look at that gal's big t—" (I punched her) —

"t-t-t-t-t-teeth."

When she was president of the Jewish Temple, Gertrude made me an honorary member. Well, I was raised a Baptist — ooh, ooh, all that water. That's why I joined the Methodists who use the sprinkling system — more my style. And now I am an honorary member of the Jewish Temple. Boy, you need all the credit cards you can get...

I was invited to Gertrude's house for seder supper; I was honored to be included... They read the passages... had a silver goblet of wine on the table for Elijah, the prophet who was supposedly taken out alive in a fiery chariot, the "Angel of the Covenant". The goblet symbolizes final redemption and Elijah would be a very welcome guest; so the front door was open for him. Gertrude said to Joe Lipshie, "Joe, go to the door and see if Elijah wants to come in." Joe got up from the table and started toward the front door.

I whispered to Gertrude, "If Elijah comes in, where would you like another door in this house?"

Following the seder, I accompanied the family to the Temple for services. I was sitting in the Kisber pew with Jonas, Jr. and Jane, Gertrude's son and daughter-in-law... the cantor had been singin' from up in the balcony, and on and on and on, went through the hyo hyo hyo hyo... I said to Jane "How many more... where are we in this thing?" Jane replied "Oh, we've got eight or ten more pages to go." I never say what I said then —"Jesus Christ!" I never, ever say that; I don't know why it rolled out of the mouth. We all got hysterical and I said "Don't knock it... He started here." Gertrude looked down at us from on high and I murmured "Shh, y'all... Gertrude's gonna throw us out of this Temple."

I was sick one year on my birthday, and couldn't make a big gala benefit "Heart Strings" dinner party, proceeds going to the Cerebral Palsy Center — Gertrude called and told me, since I couldn't make it, for my birthday she was gonna buy the 50 dollar ticket and go and have a big time in my honor. Only Gertrude...

Saturday morning about 9:00 Gertrude called and said she had not slept since 3:15... her phone rang — she got an obscene phone call. She answered the phone and he said 'I have a real hot thing for you.' And she said "Stupid me, I said 'What did you say?' I said I didn't understand him and he repeated it. Then I said 'What is your name?' And he said 'Charlie Harris.'" [right]

She hung up and didn't sleep the rest of the night... it scared her. "Well, Gertrude, I would call the Police Department and report it if you're frightened. There're a lot of things they can do..."

She called me back a few minutes later. "I forgot what he said he had for me... what was it that guy said he had for me?" "A real hot thing for you." She said "Oh yeah, okay, well, I wanted to be sure..."

She called the police and they said "What did he say?" "Well, I'm embarrassed to tell you." But she finally told them. They strongly suggested that, if she had any more calls, to inform the telephone company because they could keep check on her phone.

We were talking one night and Gertrude said "You know somethin'? It's been so long since I've been laid, I'd like to have one more big lay before I die." "Gertrude, do you ever want to?" "Oh, hell, yes." So we had sort of a running gag with Mary who said she would be our pimp; I told Gertrude she could book the Tuny Motel behind my house for a percentage.

For Gertrude: Elderly Jewish couple... Abe was having problems, went to the doctor. When he got home, his wife Sarah said "Abe, what did the doctor say?" "He said I had herpes." "What is herpes?" "I don't know, but I'll look it up in the dictionary." Abe found the word 'herpes' in the dictionary and said "Oh, Sarah, don't worry... it says here... herpes affects gentiles only."

About two weeks before she died, I went to see Gertrude. I had a little silk lei that I'd gotten in Hawaii... When I walked in I started singin' "'There she is, Miss America'... You said you wanted a good lay, and this is the best I could do." I reached down to her wheelchair and put the lei around her neck, kissed her on the cheek. She just grinned and started laughing. It was great.

She was tough; she was grand; she was class.

She was my buddy.

THE LITTLE MEETING

The First Methodist Church was having discussion home neighborhood meetings. They called and asked me if I would have a meeting here at my house, and they would give me a list of people in the surrounding neighborhood who attend our church.

What they wanted was some input about what people think we oughta do, suggestions and comments, improvements, that sort of discussion. And then we would send in our recommendations.

I said "Okay, I'll do that."

Betty Williams, who was a friend of my niece Carol, was gonna be the discussion leader and go over the information they sent out from the church. Meanwhile, I had twenty-one people to call. Out of those twenty-one, four showed up, which tickled me good 'cause I can't get a whole bunch of people in my living room anyway, with all the Tuny stuff around. So I called these people.

Well, good gracious me, ninety percent of 'em were waitresses at the Last Supper. I mean, older than God...
"Mrs. Mannix?"

"Wait a minute, honey. I've got to go get to the other phone."

"Yes, ma'am."

"Now, I can hear better. You know I can't hear too good."

"Oh, I'm sorry."

"And my eyesight's failin' me."

"Aw."

"And I'm down in my joints. Oh me, I got the arthritis in my joints and the blood ain't circulatin' in my brain too good."

I thought, God, you been dead a long time, you just don't know it, that's all.

But it was sorta funny, me talkin' to these little old people. And they had to tell me all their ailments and problems. I enjoyed it. And we had the little church meetin' here...

"They should be having two sermons on Sunday morning."

I said "Well, I wouldn't think so because he does well to get through one sometimes... But the thing about it is, you don't know how to appreciate the minister until you stand up there in that pulpit and look out over the faces you have to look at. About half of them are sittin' out there lookin' at you, sayin', Okay, let's see you git me to heaven, you think you're so good. Mercy."

Anyway, it was a useful meeting and it worked out okay. I had fun callin' all those little old people. I was kinda glad they didn't show up because I was afraid they'd fall and break their hip or something, and then sue me from hell to breakfast.

My good friend Mary told me she was walking through the Oak Court Mall in Memphis with this gal.

One of the employees of the Lord and Taylor store walked up to the woman and said "Would you like to try Calvin Klein's Eternity?"

"No, I think I'll stick with Jesus."

JUST CUZ - BEIN' TUNY

Way back when, before WDXI burned, I had a secretary, Daphne Wilkinson. Her father died and I went to the funeral, on the other side of Selmer, Tennessee. We went out to the farm, lovely farm home.

Daphne's grandmother was sitting there, cutest thing you ever saw. Sorta reminded me of Sophia on the "Golden Girls," except she had the little felt houseshoes on and a little dust cap on her head and little bitty round glasses. Couldn't hear thunder, you had to holler at her.

Daphne said "Grandma, this is Cousin Tuny."

She gave me the once-over... "Naw, you ain't Cousin Tuny."

"Yes, ma'am, I am."

"Why, Tuny, your teeth ain't out in the front."

"No, I've got my teeth in."

"Smile at me, Cousin Tuny."

And I smiled at her.

"Whew, and you got such a good fit, too. Your teeth fit so well. I wanna find out who did that."

"Well, God did that. I'm sorry."

"You mean them's your teeth?"

"Yes, ma'am, they are."

"Well, I say, don't that just beat all?"

BODY PARTS

An 80-year-old couple get married. On their way to the motel for their honeymoon, the little old bride says to the little old groom, "I think there's something I need to tell you before we get to the motel."

"Okay."

"I have acute angina."

"God, I hope so because you've got the ugliest legs I've ever seen!"

A friend asked me the other day: "Tuny, do you feel old?"

"No, I'm not old. I'm just overdosing on maturity."

I wrote this song for the older crowd... they seem to take to it — and I fit right in that category —

EVERYBODY WANTS MY BODY BUT ME

Well, ever'body wants my body but me

What is it that everyone can see?

I got a hitch in my git-along

Arthritis in my knee

To keep ever'body wantin' my body but me

I'm a sexy M and M, oh yessiree

Between Menopause and Medicare, that's me

I have flashes, flushes, aches and pains

'Specially ever' time it rains

To keep ever'body wantin' my body but me

The mileage on this model is sky-high

'Been twice around this world fast walkin' by

I'm lookin' for some trade-ins on some parts

I'll take a younger birthday, just for starts

Some things are worn and leakin'

Repairs I must start seekin'

To keep ever'body wantin' my body

Ever'body wantin' my body

Ever'body wantin' my body but me

    Hang in there, research —

To keep ever'body wantin' my body but me

THE WHITE WIDOWS

"The Wedding"

I call them the White Widows, that's b.d.o.d. — by death or divorce — they're just plain hysterical. I don't know why they invite me to things because I'm sittin' there with a bent Blue Cross card — and they've got all this Blue Chip stock and stuff and shmuck and everything. Only stock I have is a few water bugs I see every now and then... anyway, guess I sorta bring up the rear, being the youngest in the Lunch Bunch.

... There was a preacher here who was thrown out of the church because he had some affairs, they said. I don't know. But it was a big stink. His son got married and they had a major wedding... many hundreds were invited, including the White Widows...

Mary called Etta late afternoon. She thought, Well, I don't want to go to the wedding by myself. She had asked me and I told her I was going to Lexington for my executive secretary's daughter's wedding. So she called Etta.

"Etta, are you going to the wedding?"

"Yes, I'm gonna pick up Belle, so I'll just pick you up."

"Well, I'll be glad to — "

"No, let me pick you up — love for you to go with me. I'm gonna pick up Belle and I'll pick you up on the way to pick her up."

"Fine."

In the meantime, Libby calls Mary... "Mary, I'm gonna pick Pirtie and Belle up to go to the wedding, and let me pick you up."

"Well, Etta's gonna pick me up, but Etta told me she's gonna pick up Belle."

"Oh, I'll get Belle to call Etta and tell her that I'm gonna pick her up."

As Etta and Mary are heading toward Belle's house, Mary says "Libby told me that Belle was gonna call you and tell you that she was gonna go with Libby."

"I haven't heard from a soul. I said I'd pick her up, so I'm gonna pick her up."

Etta angles her big Cadillac in front of Belle's house, honks the horn — Here comes Belle... she has broken her hip and she's done real well, so out she comes with her cane.

Mary said "Belle, Libby told me she was gonna pick you up."

Belle says "I'm goin' with the person that come to get me. Y'all came first so, Etta, I'm goin' with you." She gets in the car and announces "So just go right ahead."
And they take off for the wedding.

When the ceremony's over, they go down to the big reception.

Etta comes over to Mary and Belle... "God, we got two mad women out yonder — they're madder than hell."

Mary said "Why?"

"They're blaming you, Mary."

"Blaming me for what?"

CUZ

"Well, they went by to get Belle and honked the horn and Belle didn't come. Honked again, she didn't come, so they went and knocked on the door... on the windows and everything... and she didn't come. So they swung nearby to Dr. Tyler Swindle's house [where Dr. Billy Crook used to live; really] and knocked on the door. They were having a big party. Tyler got on the phone and called Belle's son-in-law who told him where to find the key to the house... 'cause they were afraid maybe she had fallen again or something. So they got the key, went through all the house and then realized that she had already gone on ahead of 'em."

By the time Pirtie and Libby got to the church, the wedding was almost over and they had to stand out in the hall... fuming like two old wet hens. What a shame I had to miss this Medicare Mommas Mix-up.

LOUISE

If you put a mustache on Aunt Jemima on the pancake box, you'd have a likeness of Louise.

She came to work for us when Jim was about a year old. We were living in Westwood Gardens, better known as "Cardboard City." And she worked for us many, many years afterwards.

Louise had a farm, with pigs and cows, and she churned her own butter. The kids would beg her to take 'em with her when she delivered her goods to neighbors in the area... they could sit in the back of the pickup truck and laugh and have a great time.

She'd come lumberin' down the street in that truck, singin' "Swing low, sweet chariot, comin' fo' to carry me home..."

My babies were her babies.

She was always so pleasant and worked like a dog all of her life... If she don't make it to heaven, nobody else is gonna be there.

When I was pregnant with Connie, the youngest, Louise was so good to me. Of course I wouldn't take a million dollars for Connie, but I wouldn't give you a plug nickel for another'n of any kind. Connie'd be twistin' and turnin', and Louise would pick her up and put her on that big fat bosom... Connie'd just lay out. Between Lucy (as the children called her sometimes) and Mrs. Oller... Oller'd come by, open the door and say "Supper ready?" Connie would get to squirmin' and a-wigglin' back in the bedroom and Oller would go in and pick her up and bathe her. Louise was a little bit jealous of Oller and Oller was a little bit jealous of Louise.

Louise helped us move to three different houses, and she was very strong. One day I mentioned that we just had to get a new refrigerator and that I needed to get some strapping man to move the old fridge back to the garage. Came home from work; the old refrigerator was gone.

"Louise, did you find someone to move it?"

"Lawd, Miss Dorothy, I don't need no fool man to do that. I just picked it on up and put it on out there." (Geez, Louise!)

Once there was a short period of time when Louise was not available, so she had her daughter's friend, Edna, fill in for her. Edna was young, thin, attractive and good as gold. But she was scared of a storm within an inch of her life.

One night the rains came... thunder, lightning and tremendous winds. The children were sitting on the living room floor playing Monopoly, and our dog Queenie, a black mutt, was curled up there with 'em. The electricity was going off and on; the kids told me it was pretty scary... Edna freaked, grabbed Queenie in her arms and hightailed it to our next door neighbors, just a-screamin'.

The children looked at each other... about two very long minutes later, here comes Edna — knew she forgot something — and with Connie in her arms — Pat, Cindie and Jim runnin' for their drenched, monopolized lives... flat got next door to keep Queenie company.

We had trouble keeping Queenie, so when Louise came back to work, she took the dog out to her farm... way out on the highway. Two days later Queenie somehow found her way back, showed up in the front yard... waitin' for another fun storm, I suppose.

Louise cooked and cleaned and ironed beautifully, all the while singin' "Oh Lord, I'm a-goin' over yonder"... She used to stand in front of the TV when she was ironing my Tuny dresses and be sure they were ready for the show every day. We didn't have polyester then. We're talkin' about ruffle-ironin'.

And she talked to the actors on the soap operas. She knew every detail of every syrupy plot. The madder she got at them, the harder she'd iron.

"Now, Cheryl, I've told you a hunderd times... Tom ain't no good. Now git rid of him, girl. I ain't stud'in' you! Y'all just quit that!"

"And what's the matter wit you, Mona? You ain't got good sense God give a hog anyhow! You better git back to nursin' them babies, you know what's good for you. But you ain't listenin' up. Well, go ahead and mess up good, I don't care no mo' m'self. I've had it wit you and your struttin' 'round! God's gon' git you if you don't straighten up! Makes me sick to my feet!"

All the children in the neighborhood had this game they played with Louise... They'd holler "Scare us, Louise! Scare us, Lucy, pleeaase!!" Then they'd pretend they didn't know she was there and start comin' in the front door... Louise would, all of a sudden, run out the door, scream bloody murder and scare 'em so hard they'd all run in different directions down the street, panting, hearts thumpin', laughing hysterically.

CUZ

That mustache did it every time.

She didn't laugh — she cackled. When the kids ran away, Lucy'd go back to her chores shaking her head and cacklin' high and mighty... it was her game too.

The 45 Bypass went through her little farm; and it just couldn't have happened to a finer soul.

JUST CUZ - BEIN' TUNY

At General Hospital they have an annual employee picnic, when all of the administrative staff and the department directors cook and serve the 3,000 employees at the hospital.

Before I retired I was out there jumpin' and buckin' and snortin' and carryin' on with the music... singing and doin' a little entertainin' and pokin' around with 'em.

One of the employees said "Cuddin Tuny?"

"What is it, Cuz?"

"You know I loved you ever since I was a little-bitty thing. I used to watch you on the TV every evenin'. You know somethin', I bet when you pass that you gonna have the longest funeral procession ever been in all of this part of the country."

"Well, I don't know about that."

"Uh-huh, you will! When you pass, you gon' have the longest procession in these whole parts."

The more I thought about that, the funnier it got.

Thank God and Greyhound, I ain't dead yet.

THE WHITE WIDOWS

"Aw, shucks"

Belle had several of us over for dinner. She used to serve squirrel stew — her husband has been dead for many years, but he used to hunt squirrels all the time and freeze 'em. Belle would get 'em out of the freezer and make stew. Those squirrels — they'd been inanimate so many years, they'd'a grown whiskers after death.

Well, this particular evening, she served hot tamale pie... and she left the shucks on the hot tamales in the pie. I thought I would just die. I had to think of somethin' sad to keep from spewing juice... I started cuttin' into it... I thought, God, what is this? And, sure enough, it was the shucks on the hot tamales. Wonders never cease.

Thankfully, they started a conversation so I could try and get my mind off the shucks... Every time somebody'd open their mouth, somebody'd try to shut it. They were talkin' about an upcoming dance show... I call 'em the 'Medicare Recitals.' All these rich widows go to Memphis and take dancing lessons from instructors... I think they're sorta like gigolos. But, of course, it makes them happy; so that's fine. These 'recitals'... women would spend thousands of dollars for these little four-fours — they certainly couldn't get their bodies in a tutu, so you'd have to call 'em four-fours. They'd wear these costumes, and the cute little fellas would tiptoe over and do their little ta-ta's, a-one, a-two, a-three, a-four — the little old ladies would take three or four steps and they'd stop — that is, the bone would stop, but the meat on the arms would keep moving. As Agnes used to say, those dwaddles that hang off of you.

In the centerpiece on the table was a flowering quince... that's what someone said it was. It was lovely and refreshing because it had been an unusually mild January. I don't know fiddle-faddle about that subject, I am not a flower garden person. Everything my mother stuck in the ground grew pretty and bloomed, and I can't even grow artificial philodendron...

Etta said "I've got some of that blooming, too."

Blinker piped up. "I'd like to have a sprig of it."

"I'll give you a sprig, I've got a bunch of it. It's blooming in my yard. Where are you gonna put it?"

"I'm gonna put it in my yard."

"Where? In your back yard where I pick you up?"

"You don't pick me up in my back yard, that's my front yard."

"The hell you say. That is your front yard?"

"Yes."

"Well, I picked you up in the back yard."

"You picked me up in my back yard where I lived before."

"I know that, Blinker, but isn't that your back yard where I pick you up now, out there in that condo thing where you live?"

"No, that's my front yard."

"Hell, that's the most unattractive front yard I've ever seen in my life. My God, that's awful! You haven't got any place to plant anything out there! I thought the front was on the other side."

"No, that's the back."

I tried to interject — "It has a magnificent view in the back... there's glass all the way acr— "

"Well, I'll be damned. That's the damnedest thing I've ever heard — seems to me it's backwards, that's what it is, it's just backwards. I declare, that's a sight!"

I truly love the WW's, but I couldn't help thinkin' — at this moment in time — Aw, shucks... I wish I was home pickin' the lint outta my navel.

SOME GOOD GORE

Former Vice-President and Almost-President of the United States, Al Gore, is not only my cousin — he's my cousin. His mother Pauline, before marrying Senator Albert Gore, Sr., was born and bred in Jackson, along with her two brothers, Whit and "Punk," and a blind sister Thelma. Whit was a judge and Thelma ran the concession stand at the Post Office for many years. She used to come to our house when I was a little girl and visit with my sister Jenny. Mrs. LaFon, Al's grandmother and my mother's cousin, was a super-nice lady, and that's the way the whole family is.

Awhile back Jackson-Madison County General Hospital celebrated our 40th Anniversary. I invited Al to come to the awards dinner; he couldn't make it because his schedule was so hectic... we were in the middle of the Desert Storm fiasco then. But he found a way to stop by the hospital about two weeks later. It was a Wednesday morning and every Wednesday we had a Department Directors, Administrative Staff meeting... I asked Al's field rep if he could come early enough to say a few words to the Department Directors. And he did. He wanted to take a short tour of the hospital before holding a press conference in our Executive Boardroom. Then, of course, he had to head on back to Washington.

When he got there, I was waiting for him. He kissed me on the cheek... "Hello, Cousin Tuny, how are you?" Al has a lot of class. (Well, look who he's kin to — ha/ha/ha.)

Anyway, I said "Do you have any specific places you'd like to see?"

"Yeah, Tuny, I want to go to Pediatrics."

"Now you're right after my own heart because that's my baby up there."

"Great. And we'll have time to go to two other areas."

Pediatrics isn't just the pediatric wing in the hospital — it's "The Little General's Palace."

Some years ago I had a meeting with the boss, Jim Moss, and he told me he wanted a whole new concept for Pediatrics... "See what you can come up with."

About two weeks later — two o'clock in the morning — I sat straight up in bed; a light went on up in my little one cell, up above my eyes. And it dawned on me... the Little General... I just had a vision of the Little General in my mind. So I turned on the light and wrote until six o'clock. My adrenalin was pumpin', you know how it gets... a creative bug bites you and, whammo, you go crazy. I wrote a lot of stuff down and couldn't wait to get to work.

I went directly to Rosemary, Jim Moss's Administrative Assistant... "Rosemary, I've got to see Jim." And she worked me in.

"Jim, I haven't slept since two o'clock this morning."

He said "What's the matter? Are you sick?"

"Nope. I had I guess what you could call a Moss attack. That's what I call 'em. I've had these all my life. That's when, all of a sudden, the light goes on and I start writing. And here's what I think... First, we have to have a mascot. I can see a little white puppy dog with a little fat bottom in a sitting position with a sweet, satisfied smile on his face... with a little red tongue hangin' out... and give him big ears so any children who have big ears won't have such a complex... and I want him snow white, sprinkled with royal blue dots, pms 300 blue, the official color of the hospital. And I wanna call him the 'Little General.' I want to get an artist to draw him, get him manufactured, and I'll give the copyright to the hospital, from Cousin Tuny. Every child who comes into the hospital will get one of these little puppies... I want him soft and cuddly and, of course, non-allergenic. And every child will be a Little General's pal. Each pediatrician will be a character, also drawn by the artist."

Jim said "That sounds fantastic. Go with it."

So I called Joe McCormick and we met and discussed the concept. After that, it was a team effort with help from the nurses... they spend most of their lives there tending to the patients, and they also have a great sense of pride in the world we created for Pediatrics.

Once we established Little General's Palace, we started foolin' around with pet names and caricatures for the pediatricians... Kippie the Kangaroo for Kippie Miller, Walt the Wonderful for Walton Harris, Emmie the Elephant for Blanche Emerson, Robbie the Raccoon for Bob Higgs, Hoppy the Rabbit for Jimmy Hoppers, etc. Then we had an artist come in and paint caricatures and murals on the walls and doors.
We've got a mural of the Little General being weighed, taking his temperature... and in each of the rooms there's a little character that the children can see, with a picture of the Little General, along with a poem that Thelma Rushing wrote that is printed in the picture by the side of the Little General...

All the children who come in are the Little General's pals, and they can take the little puppy home with them. They hold him in their arms... gives them a sense of security, like a security blanket, while they're a patient. He's adorned with a collar that has "Little General" printed on it... such a pretty little thing.

I also said "We have no more stretchers... they're the Little

General's limousines; no more wheelchairs... they're the Little General's convertibles."

The limos and convertibles have signs on them proclaiming "Precious Cargo."

We got a Little General suit for a big person to wear, and all the children just love that big ol' dog; they really huuggg that dog.

I've loved General Hospital since the day it opened, so I'm very proud to have been able to make that contribution.

We named the restaurant downstairs in the basement "Andy's" for Andrew Jackson. There's a big mural of Andrew Jackson and scenes from Tennessee on the walls. The cafeteria on the first floor is named "Rachel's" for Andy's wife. So it all blends in with Jackson-Madison County General Hospital... works out real well.

Little General has brought a lot of happiness and eased a lot of pain for many children... soothed 'em down and helped them get rid of their fears...

After we toured Pediatrics, I took Al to our Rehabilitation unit, where the stroke and accident victims are.

We had time to go to one more place, and I said "Al, I wanna take you down in the trenches where the General's real heroes are. The nurses help make it happen too, of course, but I wanna take you to a special place." He said "Lead on, Tuny."

We were on the fourth floor, so we got on the elevator and went all the way down to the basement. Between the main hospital building and another building which is about half a block or more away, there is a tunnel underneath the street that leads to the laundry. And that tunnel is hotter than a firecracker in a barrel o' snakes.

I took all those people... entourage... television cameras, newspaper reporters, Jim Moss, the top echelon... Here we go tricklin' down through the tunnel, with big ol' steampipes up in the ceiling...

I walked into the laundry and hollered "A future President of the United States [little did I know] is here to hug everybody in this place because you're so important and we love you."

It thrilled those people to death. And Al hugged every one of 'em. We took some pictures, trickled back through the tunnel, and on to the boardroom.

He put his arms around me and said "Tuny, thank you, thank you."

I said "Let me tell you somethin', cuz, those people down there are gonna be on the front seat in heaven and I'm gonna be tryin' to get under the gate. They're good, God-fearing, God-lovin' folks and they work like dogs. And there but for the grace of God be me or mine... I look up to them because they are the kind o' people who really make the wheels turn... the people in the laundry, in the kitchen, the ones with mops cleanin' up all the messes."

'Course everybody's my cousin. But Al's one of my honest-to-goodness cousins, and I am so proud of him.

FULL CHICKEN COLONEL

In 1958, Ernest Frankland was the Commanding General of the Tennessee National Guard. He was one of the highest decorated, besides Jack Holland, of our Jacksonians from World War II. They had an encampment once a year; and this particular year it was in Fort Stewart, Georgia. They would invite VIP's down for the weekend for the big review.

Ernest asked me if I would come down, and a paratrooper plane picked me up at the airport here. I got on this big ol' plane that Saturday morning... you had to sit in the bucket. And there's one set of bunk beds. I had on a white helmet with "Cousin Tuny" in gold letters across it, baby blue pedal pushers and white Oxford shoes.

We flew from Jackson to Nashville and landed at Berry Field, where we were pickin' up some VIP's. I had had a Coke and my eyeballs were floatin', so I was tryin' to find the rest room 'cause we were gonna be there about 30 minutes. They wanted to know if I wanted some coffee; I thought 'Lord no, these aren't tears in my eyes from layin' on my back and cryin' on you!' My puckerin' string was about to explode. They told me to go up these stairs and down this hall — it was so quiet, everything was closed down.

I opened a door and this Lieutenant was sitting behind a desk. I said "Oh, excuse me, I was looking for the powder room."

"It's right behind this office."

So I went in and closed the door. It was so quiet I could

hear that officer writing with a soft lead pencil. And I'm sittin' there thinkin', what am I gonna do? I started singin' "The Tennessee Waltz." Sang it through twice... I was in pretty bad shape.

When I came out, he said "I wish I was going to Fort Stewart with you."

"Well, I wish you were too. Thanks so much, and I thank God I knew 'The Tennessee Waltz' all the way through." [I don't know about me and bathrooms... the strangest things seem to happen]

We got back on the plane and started off — went to Chattanooga to pick up some VIP's before we flew on down to Fort Stewart, Georgia. I was sittin' there talkin' to the Mayor from Milan, Tennessee, who was sittin' on the bottom berth of the bunks. All of a sudden, the plane hit an air pocket and it dipped; when it did, the back of his head hit the bottom of the top bunk bed — his hairline dropped. It's kinda strange when you're talkin' to somebody and suddenly their hairline drops all the way to just above their eyebrows.

He said "Oh my God, my new toupée — I just put it on today."

"I'm glad you told me that. I was about to think I was goin' crazy here."

I was the only woman on the plane when we arrived at Fort Stewart... they radioed ahead and said "We want Cousin Tuny to deplane first." So when they landed at the air base, opened the door and rolled those steps up, I stepped out. I looked up and here came Ernest Frankland and Joe Henry, the Adjutant General of the State of Tennessee, and all these high moguls drippin' in brass, and the full band. They started playin' "Dixie." There were some real important people on that plane — I was just the peon — but since I was the girl, I guess they let me out first...

I sang "Sweet Georgia Brown" with the band at a big party that night. The next morning a special car picked me up at my motel about ten miles from the base and brought me to the review. I sat right behind Governor Frank Clement and Adjutant General Joe Henry and General Ernest Frankland... I'm a VIP-er. It was really quite impressive... they had some people from Washington and Senators and all that jazz, and a huge crowd to watch the review.

I was invited over to the Adjutant General's headquarters for lunch... dressed normally this time, fit to kill. Went over there for some drinks, and the Aide carried me out to the motel so I could put on my pantaloons; and I came back and entertained the luncheon; that was really fun, singin' some songs for 'em and doin' a little standup comedy.

I have a swagger stick hanging in my sitting room that's engraved, from Frank Clement. I was given a certificate and made an Honorary Colonel in the Tennessee National Guard.

When we were to leave for the plane to fly back, they put me in one of Ernest Frankland's old uniforms — 'course I looked like a family of younguns had moved out of the seat of my britches — decorated me and put the chicken colonel things on that uniform somethin' fierce — then they put the chicken colonels on my helmet.

I started to get in the car and Mason Brown, who was Lieutenant Colonel in the Tennessee National Guard, was to ride with me. In a military car, the person that is highest-ranked sits on the right side, to the right of the driver in the back seat, not behind the driver. I was gettin' in the left and he said "Uh-uh, uh-uh, Tuny... I'm a Lieutenant Colonel, you're full chicken, you're full Colonel... you get over there in that seat where the high rank sits."

Talk about an exhilarating weekend!

SPACED OUT

I had the privilege of being among 29 women, all affiliated with American Women in Radio & Television, selected to go on an orientation tour of the Space Centers through the Air Force. We all met on June 20th, 1967, at Berry Field in Nashville; and went by bus to Arnold Engineering Development Center in Tullahoma, Tennessee, where we were briefed and then toured this tremendous operation. After being dinner guests of General Gossick, Commander of Arnold, we spent the night at a motel in Tullahoma. We left by Air Force plane the next morning for Dobbins Air Force Base in Marietta, Georgia, and were carried by bus to Lockheed for briefing and a tour.

A young man hopped aboard the bus and introduced himself as Roy Simmons, the Director of Marketing and Public Relations for Lockheed:

"Unfortunately, I do not have the time to do these tours, due to other pressing priorities; but I have a fabulous staff who can really do a better job than I can. However, when I looked over the list of VIP's with our group and saw Cousin Tuny's name, I knew I would have to drop everything and do this one myself. You see, I am from Henderson, Tennessee, and I've worshipped this lady all my life... and my parents would not let me in the house when I visit them if I had neglected to personally take care of Cousin Tuny and her special cousins."

Well... how I felt... it was so touching. He personally invited me to come down to be in the big VIP Circle three months from then, when they were going to have the roll-out of the big C-5A plane and President Lyndon Johnson was going to be there.

I would have been able to interview the President. Couldn't get my expenses paid for, so it didn't work out. But it was superfine to be invited.

The tour at Lockheed included going through the plywood replica of the largest plane in the world, that was to become a reality in spring of '68... the C-5A, that can handle eight Greyhound busses end to end on the lower floor... yes, there is an upstairs with all the comforts of a hotel. This was really something. We had lunch at Lockheed, courtesy of the Commandant, and Dr. Switzer from Oak Ridge sat at my left... General McConnell was there, along with the top brass from the British Air Command.

We boarded our U.S. Air Force plane and took off for Patrick Air Force Base, Florida, where we were met by Colonel Ledford and were his guests at dinner. We spent the night in the motel there and next morning boarded our bus for Cape Kennedy Air Force Station for briefing and toured the Complex 26, Space Museum, and the Titan III C Complex. From there we were off to John F. Kennedy Space Center, NASA, and were briefed and toured the NASA Moonport, Complex 39. We saw all the launching pads, of course, and spent some time at the pad where we would shoot for the moon in 1970. Got a good look at the lunar module that landed our astronauts. We were toured by the Colonel into the Control Centers at NASA, and then boarded our plane for Kelly Air Force Base, San Antonio, Texas. Another bus carried us to headquarters, Aerospace Medical Division, Brooks Air Force Base, where we were briefed and toured the USAF School of Aerospace Medicine by General Roademan and Colonel Glasgow. This included the tanks used in simulation, for this is where the astronauts are evaluated and where they take a great deal of their training. The tour was over on June 23rd, and we landed back at Berry Field.

There are really no words to express what this tour did to

me. Of course, we had gobs of fun; and yours truly entertained two nights. I helped land the plane at Patrick Air Force Base, with famous words like "Patrick baby, we want to land our big old bird in your li'l ole front yard."

We were privileged to meet some of the greatest scientists and leaders in our world today, and on board we had Senator Mary Anderson from Nashville and Commissioner Josephine Berson, so I was in the middle of brass all the way.

When we stood at the pad where the three astronauts were killed, we were in silence for a moment... we realized history was made here and these boys gave their lives for a secure future for their country... And we were also in the midst of history-making events. We were badged; had to check all cameras; however, the Air Force took pictures of us (Gosh, mine might end up in the Post Office; I'd prefer a stamp to a Wanted poster, thank you very much).

THE AMERICAN FLAG

Every American needs to go around Pearl Harbor. As you sail around the harbor, you see this big white monument looming in the distance... as you get closer, you realize that it is the monument built over the sunken USS Arizona, the battleship that went down with 1200 men aboard; and they're still down there because the current is too swift; they lost several frogmen who went down trying to get some of the bodies up, so it was decided to let those boys stay in that grave together. I was so moved. All of the names are deeply carved in this white monument.

And you can see the bow of the ship... there's a big flagpole and at the top of that huge, long, tall flagpole Old Glory is flying at full mast. I saw the rusted hull of the USS Tennessee... naturally, that put a little lump in my throat...

A voice came out over the loudspeaker, sounded like John Nesbitt's Passing Parade voice, in a very respectful, soft tone... "Ladies and gentlemen, you will notice that Old Glory is flying at full mast over the sunken USS Arizona. Below are 1200 boys who gave their lives on December 7th, 1941. And Old Glory will always fly at full mast because those boys below us will always be in full service of their country."

That really did something to me. You know that you're on hallowed waters... those boys went down for our flag, for what it stands for. When our Supreme Court handed down that it was perfectly alright for some turkey to burn the American flag, I was appalled.

I disagree in desecrating the flag, which is a symbol of the unity of this country. What he thinks is one thing, but when you start desecrating something, you're gettin' into <u>my</u> First Amendment. I mean, I have some rights too.

True, it's just a piece of cloth... well, the Cross is just a piece of wood, too. But it's the symbol... what it stands for. I feel like anybody who wants to burn the American flag needs to get the hell out of America. Either love it or leave it. There're a lot of places for them to go. There are no chains attached to them. But thank God people rallied to the cause. And they'll always rally to the cause because of what that flag stands for. To destroy it is demeaning, defacing and, to me, it is blasphemous.

THE SILENT MAJORITY

Hey, you, there in the street

With your signs, your screams, your marching feet

You're missing the boat, man

You're ruining the scene

You'll never make the grade on that losing team

You say you want peace

Well, don't everybody, son?

And what do you have when your destroying is done?

Well, you have a symbol of violence, lust and greed

And that's not the way to fill the peace need

You say you're doing your thing

Your country not to shirk

But how many times have you done an honest day's work?

And how do you think the world got this far?

Certainly not by destroying things as they are.

The thing to do to make these things improve

Is to get with it, son, get in the right groove

To wipe out all your hate and wrath

First you need to take a real good bath

Cleanse your body, your soul, your mind and your heart

Then, son, you're ready to really take heart

Don't pledge your fist and hold it in the air

Just place your hand over your heart

And say a prayer

Yes, son, you see, God is on our side

We march with our Bible and Old Glory with pride

And our team's the winner, it'll always be

For all races working together

We'll always be free

So if you really want peace in the world today

Join us, we're the real USA

cuz

And we'd like you to join us, and if you wanna shout

Shout God Bless America, for this right will out

If you're determined to continue to fight what is true

Then all I can is, son, God have mercy on you.

On July 4th, 1989, I watched the Capitol 4th celebration on TV... it was on the lawn of the Capitol in Washington. Pearl Bailey opened it up with the "National Anthem" and Peter Nero played George Gershwin's "Rhapsody In Blue" with the National Symphony Orchestra — just fantastic.

I reflected on the year before, when I was in Washington at the meeting of the American Hospital Association, Marketing and Public Relations Directors from all over the United States... and we drove by the Vietnam Memorial. We stopped for awhile...

I saw mothers, wives, fathers, brothers and sisters of those guys who died in Vietnam. And those names were engraved in that dark black marble.

I noticed one woman in particular... and I know she had to be the mother of that boy. She was standing there and her fingers were gently and lovingly moving over his name, each engraved letter... I thought, that's all she has... his name up there with all those thousands of others.

SPECIAL SOMETHING

I've got myself a something, a super-special something

That keeps me up and going every day

It's my love and dedication to this, my American nation

This great magnificent wonderful USA

I make an honest living, to my country I'll be giving

My full support just like it oughta be

I vote in each election, try to make the best selection

To represent and speak for you and me

For all our problems, there's the right solution

It's working to uphold our Constitution

So get yourself this something, this super-special something

That's real America working every day

With love and dedication to our great American nation

That's the all red, white and blue — the USA

That's the great, the true, the real American way

BEAUTY IS DEEP

In the early days of the Miss Tennessee Pageant, I ran up and down the streets selling it to advertisers in pieces, wrote the commercials, and sat in Rothrock Stadium in the rain and heat interviewing the contestants and broadcasting the proceedings. Months before the Pageant, I sent out press releases across the state and talked to all the newspapers, TV and radio stations... This involvement led to emceeing preliminary pageants throughout the state.

I wrote a song to help loosen up the proceedings and just have fun with the audience... then I'd segue into a number about our glorious state...

>I have seen girls, onstage and backstage too
>
>Yet I can't contest, even tho' I'm a girl too...
>
>Now just 'cause their framework is built like brick
>
>Well, mine's just like brick too
>
>'Course my mortar is sorta loose, you see,
>
>What am I to do?
>
>When these contestants smile, the sun shines thru
>
>I open my mouth and there's a gap clean thru
>
>Oh, my spring is sprung, my youth is wrung
>
>That ugly stick done hit me

Now this model ain't so, well, not real, real old

But there's too much mileage, I've been told

My gears are shot, my youth is spent

My get-up-and-go has done got up and went

But I'll be content with this here model

I'll keep smilin', gap and all

'Cause my heart's gonna stay so bright and lovely

Big as a treetop tall

You see, I love my state, yessirree,

Gonna sing a song for you and me

For the greatest state

I'll sing it now, my home state Tennessee...

<u>T</u> is for the treetops, the greenest in the land

<u>E</u> means that it's easy to live where folks are grand

Double <u>N</u> means there's nothin' north of the

Mason-Dixon Line

That can compare to when I'm there where I keep this heart of mine.

<u>E</u> means that I'm eager to be back home once more

cuz

Double <u>S</u> means that someone sweet will greet me at the door

The last two <u>E</u>'s mean each and everyone must now agree...

That <u>T</u> <u>E</u> double <u>N</u> <u>E</u> double <u>S</u> double <u>E</u> spells Tennessee...

And that spells heaven to me!

One night in Johnson City I dropped all my cards... danced and sang while I was picking them up. That smoothed out okay... until... the electricity went off — all that was left was one spotlight. I was standin' there in front of two thousand people. Most of the orchestra was electric. I looked down and saw trumpets, drums, and a piano.

"Alright, guys, I want you to give me some good kind a' dancin' music."

They let loose and so did I. Thank goodness I didn't have to do but a few minutes... it kinda takes the wind out of you to dance hard and then emcee.

I managed to muddle through... until... it was time to ask the semi-finalists questions... the judges forgot to put the questions together, so I had to make them up off the top of my head.

Some of the hardest ones to emcee are children's pageants. Those poor little mommas standin' out there in raggedy clothes so that their five-year-old little girl can have a hundred dollar dress to be in a beauty pageant.

I was one of the judges for a children's pageant — ninety-eleven children, girls and boys. We picked out a Queen and a King...

The next night they were having the senior pageant, with just female contestants. Gertrude Kisber was with me, and we were in the audience. Seated in front of us was this couple...

The man kept sayin' "You're not gonna do it."

"Yes I am..." The woman turned around and said "Cousin Tuny."

"Yes."

Her hair was bloodred, freckles all over her face... "My little girl was in that pageant last night and she was the prettiest one up there, and I wanna know why she didn't win."

I remembered a little fat girl — I thought she was a doll — with freckles and bloodred hair — who came waddlin' out there on the stage.

I smiled at the mother and said "Was your daughter that precious little girl with the red hair and freckled face?"

"Yes."

"Well, I voted for her. But all those other judges voted against me."

She flashed a grin and elbowed her husband... "I told you Tuny'd vote for her, I told you she would. She'd've given it to her if she could've. Yessir, I knew you'd do that, Tuny, 'cause you know beauty when you see it."

"Oh, yessiree bobolinko, I surely do."

You know, it's dangerous. I made up my mind then, that's the last one I judge. I tell ya, those mommas will unscrew your navel and let your legs fall off. I mean, they're out there for blood. Every crow thinks theirs is the blackest, and that's the way it should be. That's nature. But no more of that for this beauty.

cuz

Somehow, I've bluffed my way through — thanks to my guardian angel up there.

MY MAN

Just for kicks, I bought a new sheet... it's white satin with a gorgeous hunk o' man on one side — happens to be the side where I sleep. He's wearing a jockey bikini, looks like he's about 29 years old... about my speed. He's lyin' there on his back with his hands under his head, full-length. I had it stretched out on the bed one day when Pat dropped by.

"Pat, I want you to meet my new boyfriend." And I brought her in my bedroom — she just fell out.

"When I die, I want you to say 'Cousin Tuny was found dead in bed on top of a good-lookin' man.'"

My first grandson, Stephen, was working part-time at Kroger grocery store then; and Pat said "I've got to go by Kroger and tell Stephen. I'm gonna tell him that you wanna see him after work."

"Stephen, your grandmother has a new boyfriend."
"You're kiddin' me."

"No, she has a new boyfriend and she wants you to meet him."

"Mom, do I know him?"

"No, you don't know him."

"Would you go out with him?"

"Sure would. But you know I wouldn't cross your grandmother, that's one person I wouldn't cross."

So Stephen came over and I said "Well, he's in the

bedroom." He turned so red.

When I showed him the sheet, he said "I knew there was some sort of catch to it."

"How do you know? I might have a good-lookin' young man in here; you never can tell. I'm that cute."

"Of course you're that cute, Grandmother."

You've got to do little things sometimes... you can get dull and old if you just sit around and let it happen to you... no way for this José...

JUST CUZ - BEIN' TUNY

I got a call that T.G. Sheppard, the country singer, was in the hospital visiting his father who had had surgery. T.G.'s bus was parked out in front of the hospital and was causing a good bit of commotion. I was told they put the family in the consultation room outside Intensive Care because he's such a public figure.

As I passed the regular waiting room that has glass all across the front, there were about twenty people in there and I waved at 'em; they looked and waved back. I zipped around the corner and stood in the door. "T.G.?"

"Lord have mercy, Tuny!" He got up, came over, hugged and kissed me... I hadn't seen him in several years... He said "You haven't changed a bit."

"Don't get your eyes examined, cuz, just keep on talkin' like that 'cause I love it, I love it."

His father had cancer surgery, but they thought they got it all. He said he'd just done a couple of weeks in Vegas and was on his way to Birmingham, Alabama to do a TV special. And I gave the family some tokens for the parking lot.

As I came back around by the waiting room, all these people were at the entrance to the doorway going into the Intensive Care consultation room. One of 'em said "You are Cousin Tuny, aren't you?"

"Yes, I am."

"Lord, would you come in here a minute?"

I thought, oh my, we got a problem here, because they called me when they had problems so much of the time. I walked in and said "What can I do for you?"

"We want your autograph."

And they started rippin' off these little pieces of paper for me, to say 'to Billy Bob' and 'to Christie' and 'Mindy' and 'for Mary Sue' and 'to Betty Jo'... most of 'em were on my TV show when they were little. They all hugged me... it was real sweet.

I said "Do you realize that T.G. Sheppard is in the hospital?"

"Yeah, we know that. We'd ruther see you first. Then if we can see him, okay; but if not, we just had to be able to see you 'cause we love you so."

"Well, you don't know what you've done to me; you've made my whole week."

When I came out of the waiting room, standin' in the hall, T.G. appeared around the corner. "Tuny, what you up to?"

"Signing autographs. I just want to tell you that you're nothing."

"Well, when you're around, Tuny, I know I'm nothing."

Everybody got a kick out of that. Mercy me.

THE WHITE WIDOWS

"Sustuh"

Here I was, resting in bed, recuperating from surgery, when 'Sustuh' called... "Dawrriss, how-aare-yuu?? This is Mimi Watlington."

I started to say 'Honolulu, how-aare-<u>yuu</u>?' "Hello, Mimi. I'm fine. I just read in the paper that John, Jr.'s going to marry Carolyn."

"Ohhh, yess, I'm soo excited! I'm flying to the South of France for the wedding... I'm in Phoenix, you know, in my home in Phoenix, Arizona, calling you long dissstance."

"Oh, that's nice."

"Have you been sick?"

"No, just had surgery; but I'm doin' okay."

"I want to ask a favor of you. I was gonna fly out of here Saturday morning, but <u>I</u> just got an invitation to <u>the</u> pawrty of the season."

I thought, Oh, Sustuh, ha-ha-ha...

"And the pawrty... I mean, everybody of everybody... they're going to be there. It's a 'Tacky Party' — and I wanted to borrow one of your Cousin Tuny outfits."

I said "I beg your pardon."

"Oh, well, I would tell them that this is what a big TV star in Jackson, Tennessee wears."

"Mimi, I've been off for almost eight weeks, and I knew I was going to be out of commission for a good while; so, before I had surgery, my maid Jessie packed up all my Tuny costumes and they're sealed in a box in the attic."

"Ohh, I'll send Curtis [her servant] over and he can go up there and get 'em."

"No, he can't, because I can't make the stairs."

"Well, he can go up there and bring each box down."

"Mimi, he can't do that. It's very hot in the attic, and I don't even know which box they're in. I'm sorry."

"Oh, well, what will I dooo?"

"I would suggest you look in the Yellow Pages under Costume Stores; I'm sure they must have one in Phoenix or Tucson."

"Oh, I hadn't thought of that... I _do_ hope you get along alright. 'Byyee...'"

Sustuh!! That's like asking for your heart or your liver or your lung, and you try to keep on livin'. It is to me. Ask me anything, but don't ask for my Tuny outfit.

What price glamour.

MAKING RIGHT

Stepping into the sleepy town of Fulton, Kentucky, 65 miles up 45 North Highway, is like stepping into another realm. It's a different world up there.

Fulton High School usually has a reunion every year. In 1990, it was bigger than before, combining 1940-43 classes, mine being '42... about 150 people were there altogether, and that's a big crowd. It was wonderful. I jitterbugged my britches off. Most of my classmates don't jump around as much as I do. Maybe they haven't been as hungry as I have, to get out and hump those bushes to make next week's groceries... I saw a coupla old boyfriends and I'm glad I didn't marry them.

There were 13 parties from Thursday morning early through Saturday night — I never partied so much in my life, and I didn't miss one of 'em — had a ball! Friday morning I had a coupla hours free... I picked up the phone and called my stepsister. Mary Louise Warren is twelve years older than I am, and she was already married and gone from home when I went to Fulton in 1940.

"Mary Louise, this is Doris."

"Doris! It's so nice to hear from you. I heard you were comin' to Fulton... how are you doing?"

"Just fine. I would like to come by and see you for a few minutes."

"Oh, that would be great! I have a luncheon at 11:30, but I'll be home 'til then."

I rang the doorbell. When she came to the door, I hugged

her neck and followed her inside... I'm sure she was a little bit uncertain... not really knowing why I was there. We sat down and chatted for awhile... I showed her a picture of my children... She said "You know, I watch you on the telethons and I'm real proud of what you've done, Doris."

"Mary Louise, the main reason why I came by here... I haven't seen you in 40 years, except at Betty Lou's funeral last year, just briefly. I wanted to tell you something. You were good to me. You were kind to me. You taught me to drive when I was 15 years old, and you helped me pull out of several situations. I wanted you to know that I appreciated it, and I admire and respect you... I want to give everybody their roses while they can still smell them."

I didn't pursue that any further. She never mentioned her mother's name and neither did I... but that night of my Queen's Ball, when my stepmother made me leave and embarrassed me so... it's not easy to erase.

I wanted Mary Louise to know that I had not forgotten her kindness. I think my real mother would have been proud of me, and I know Agnes would have been... 'cause I stood up a little bit taller.

Made me feel good all over.

1,000 POINTS OF LIGHT

This was the phrase our elder President Bush used to describe America's volunteers. It was a total surprise to me to be chosen as one of the Thousand Points of Light. Mary Frances Christie, my Assistant Director of Marketing and Public Relations at General Hospital, nominated me and sent some information on me to the <u>Commercial Appeal</u> in Memphis. That's how I got selected. They had a write-up in the <u>Commercial</u> on each one of us and the President was coming to Memphis to honor these fifty people.

Jackie, Mary Frances' husband who works for the state, took the day off to drive us to Memphis. And it rained, rained, rained and rained. Why does it rain every time I leave town??

The ceremony was held outside, and they would not let you take an umbrella in there. We were searched with one of those electrical things to make sure we didn't have any metal, and Secret Servicemen were all over the place. We sat there in the pouring down rain and, par for the course, the President was late.

Since it was raining when we left for Memphis, I grabbed three big plastic trash bags and put 'em down for us to sit on. It did not stop raining. We sat on one of the bags and split the other two and wrapped up in them. The President finally spoke and commended us...

When we got in the car and started back on I-40, I said "You'all, we're gonna stop here at this mall and have lunch and I've got to buy something to put on because, Mary Frances, you and I both are gonna be sick." I was drippin' wet clear through my trench coat, my suit, all the way to my skin. So we both bought warm-up suits and put them on.

I said "We're sittin' there in this pouring down rain for the President of the United States to walk up here and tell us how great we are — and we may die of pneumonia before we get home."

Sure, it's exciting to be honored by the President... but you don't volunteer for charity work or visit sick children or help with telethons to get recognition.

You do it to give your soul a bath.

THE CEREBRAL PALSY CENTER
"God's Special Children"

God's Special Children
They're growing each day
Each one progressing in his own special way
Although they know what to expect
Just to survive
These precious faces still reflect
The joy of being alive

> Their kind of patience and courage
> I wish I possessed
> They meet each day with a smile
> In your every test
> Putting their trust in us
> Never seeing our faults
> Accepting without question
> What their lives have wrought
>
> Oh yes, there's a limit to what they can do
> But there's no limit on their love
> Oh, it comes shining through
> So it's only fair that we share
> We should not need a shove
> These are God's Special Children
> And they sure deserve our love

This poem was written by Sylvia Crumby in Michie, Tennessee. I set it to music and sing it during the annual Cerebral Palsy Telethon which we broadcast on WBBJ-TV. In the early sixties, I was asked to help start a Cerebral Palsy Center in Jackson. I said "What is Cerebral Palsy?" I had seen children with it, but didn't realize what it was.

"It's an injury to the motor nerve to the brain. It can happen from an accident, or it can happen at birth."

So we started in a little house behind a house in a lady's back yard on North Royal Street, in two little rooms... we had four children... those children are dead now, they were severely involved.

The Cotillion Club adopted the Cerebral Palsy Center as their main charity and I don't know what we would have done without them. They helped us move out of those two rooms into another house that we rented until they sold the house... we didn't have the money to buy it. Forest Heights Methodist Church let us have space over there. We had one room and had to use everything the church had, except for some special chairs and some of our special toys. Jean McCoy, who became Director of the Center, shared an office with a church employee — didn't even have a desk — that's how destitute we were... until they built the Robert J. Smith Developmental Complex on Garland Drive. That was thanks to Dr. Bob Smith... he went to Nashville and Washington, got matching funds... and the CP Center finally found a home in 1977. Others have helped, too, most notably Walter Baker Harris. But Bobby Joe Smith held free clinics every month — he would come out and see children from all over the West Tennessee area, absolutely free. And do evaluations, make recommendations for bracing, etc.... he was and is our guiding light.

We were affiliated with United Cerebral Palsy during the first telethon in 1966. Later we pulled away from them and incorporated here. I became very involved working with the telethons then, and with the Board of Directors, eventually becoming Board Chairman for a couple of years.

The telethons began in a high school, and moved on to the Civic Center as expenses soared through the roof. Wink Martindale, veteran radio and television personality, hosted for a good many years. The telethon was in his name, being from Jackson, and he brought in entertainment from the West Coast. When he was here, I was in charge of all the activities involved with the children. The overhead got out of hand and we lost our main focus a bit, so we had to bring it back home, to a local level. Wink did a tremendous thing for the Center. And we certainly wouldn't be out there and where we are now if it hadn't been for him. Whenever I'm speaking to a group about the Cerebral Palsy Center, I try to bring this out, because it's so true. Wink gave of his time and energies for this heartrending cause.

We've had many stars come in over the years... naturally, a lot of country music stars; but also a good variety from the West and East Coasts... Johnny Mathis, Tex Ritter, Maureen McGovern, The Lettermen, Foster Brooks, Fred Travalena, Robert Urich, etc.... most important to us, my good friend Carl Perkins, the 'King of Rockabilly,' Mr. 'Blue Suede Shoes,' another native Jacksonian. Since we curbed the big-star overhead and brought it back home where it belongs, I emceed and Carl helped me host the telethons. No cue cards — just doing it. We have so much local talent, terrific entertainers like Debbie Kincaid Gooch, The Long Brothers and my daughter Connie... it works out beautifully... for the children, and that's what it's all about.

We must be doing something right... Gene Evans, who used to live in Hollywood as a producer, came to Jackson to appear on the telethon and wound up living here... he'd always wanted a log cabin. So Gene appears with me every year, too. He's a great addition to our heartfelt teamwork for God's Special Children. With our local clubs and organizations, like the Old Hickory Rotary Club and our sponsor from the beginning, the Cotillion Club, we get by and keep on keepin' on. All the money people pledge stays here for the children at the Cerebral Palsy Center... we've finally gotten to the point where we're underwritten before we go on the air, through our sponsors, corporations here in town.

Wink Martindale and Jean McCoy were on the air talking about the benefits of water therapy, how the cerebral palsy children can move in the water when they can't move outside the water, and what a great exercise it is for them. After the broadcast, Jean got a call from a man who said he'd been watching and wanted to know how much a therapy pool like that would cost. After several conversations, this anonymous person, our CP Angel, gave the Center 200,000 dollars for the pool. It is one of twenty in the country... has a hydraulic floor, operated from a panel, where you can roll the children out onto the floor and float 'em out of their chair. This became a reality that we could hardly believe. Our angel called Jean sometimes to talk about the Center and what's happening there. The year Jean retired he gave 25,000 dollars, in her honor. I presented "Our Special Friend" with a plaque during one of the telethon broadcasts... At his request he remained anonymous until his death a few years ago... He was Mr. Glen Dillon, now reaping his rewards in paradise!

Tuny and Gene Evans

Telethon, finale, including Connie Freeman, Tuny's daughter

Tuny and Carl

CUZ

An idea I had for a "Chosen Child" project has worked out nicely... and the Old Hickory Rotary Club rose to the cause... to sponsor a child. It costs eleven thousand dollars plus to educate a child per year... physical therapy, speech therapy, the whole spectrum. That's high in relation to what there's actually being spent on "normal" kids. Not only clubs like Kiwanis and civic clubs around town do this, businesses and individuals join in too — God knows, anyone is welcome. Another dream becomes reality.

The late Steve Long - helping God's Special Children

"Tuny's Cousins" is a large caricature drawing of my character — the face. We ask people to call in and pledge ten dollars a month for a year to become a Tuny's Cousin... we put their name on a strip of stickum paper and plaster those names all around the drawing of my face... so far, so good... we've 'covered me up' every year.

The small gifts are the ones that mean so much because people usually have to do without something in order to make that contribution. Miss Ouida Scroggins, on Social Security, called and told us she is putting away a dollar every week, in her purse that she keeps on top of the television. I have Miss Scroggins on the telethon every year to present her 52 dollars. It's the little man that counts.

To give these children a better quality of life... I tell the TV audience... we are our brother's keeper... Make a rainbow and you'll have a pot of gold... gold of love, caring, hope. It gives you contentment and self-esteem, and the Good Lord will take a likin' to you. One somebody carries a feather bed up a flight of stairs, it's a chore... but if a whole lot of people carry a few feathers, it's a piece of cake. You show everybody how your momma raised you, and your life will be happier.

We have a Christmas party for the children at the Center... Several years ago, after the party, I went by the hospital and visited with a girl who was dying of esophageal cancer. Twenty years before, she was seven, with cerebral palsy, and I walked across the stage of the first telethon with her. All her pain is gone now.

There was an eight-year-old boy, blond, cute as a button, who was on my TV show when we were broadcasting from the theatre... From the stage, I could see he had a problem because he was walking with metal crutches. I jumped down and went up the aisle to him, but he came up the stage steps himself.

I said to his mother... "Will you tell me about him before I go on the air with him?"

"Oh yes. He was born without arms and without legs. He has artificial arms, hooks for hands, and artificial legs."

"Does he mind talking about it?"

"Oh no. He'd love to show you how to turn pages with the hooks. He's proud of what he can do... and he has something he wants to do especially for you."

I interviewed him and he showed how he could turn pages.

"Okay, little cousin, are you gonna perform for us or are you gonna be entertained?"

"I'm gonna perform. I have to go all the way across the stage, and I want you to stand here."

"Alright... Cameras move back so we can get this big performance."

He moved the crutches across the stage, turned around and said "Are you ready?"

"I'm ready."

He dropped one crutch, then he dropped the other crutch, and that child walked across that stage on those artificial legs to me, and put those little artificial arms around me. I melted in the floor.

There wasn't a dry eye in the control room... those hard-noses in there doin' the switcher and directing the show... it was a wonderful thing.

And that little boy grew up, went to college and got married. He teaches art in the Lexington, Tennessee school system. He paints beautifully by holding the brush between his teeth... His name is Lonnie Williams — a real sweetheart!

Somebody starts bitchin' about something they can't do, you want to hit 'em in the mouth.

During the 1978 telethon, a beautiful ten-year-old girl sang a song... she had a good country music voice. Unfortunately, this precious little girl was blind.

After her performance, I saw her backstage. She said "Cousin Tuny, this is the first time I have met you."

"Would you like to see what I look like?"

She smiled real big and said "Oh, yes..."

I took her hands and started at the daisy (antenna) on top of my hat, down through the freckles, blacked-out teeth, dress, pantaloons, socks and high-top shoes. She lit up like a neon sign which, of course, melted me down to a puddle.

This particular year my youngest, Connie, was here to entertain at the telethon... I had no idea she was in the wings watching my meeting with the little blind girl. The next morning I went to work, leaving Connie to sleep late before her trek back to Nashville. When I got home that day, there was a poem in Connie's handwriting on the kitchen table...

The Inspiration of 4-30-78

A little hand on a pantaloon,

Seeing what eyes cannot,

Upon the knee of a special soul,

Who gives with all she's got...

Among the midst of stops and starts,

She takes the time to kneel,

And show a little hand and heart

How to see by 'feel'...

cuz

It matters not her 'cousin's' size,

Or shape in which he's born,

Behind that freckled face disguise,

She lights up those who mourn!

Through all the years I've watched her steps...

Moving to many tunes,

But never a step sent such love to my heart

As that hand on the pantaloon!

One year I was singing "Jesus Loves Me" to little Michelle, six years old, the "CP Child" for the telethon. She looked up at me from her wheelchair with big, loving eyes, smiled, reached over and held on to my hand. It was magnificent...

Talking and singing with the CP children is the most heartwarming part of it all. We sing songs like "Side By Side" and "Have Faith, Hope and Charity" that we used to sing on my TV show. That's when the phones really ring off the wall.

These experiences humble you, and we need a dose of that ever so often. It's heavy stuff... you feel about 50 feet tall and, at the same time, like a speck on a wall. Everybody deserves a fair shake in life. And these, God's Special Children, certainly deserve even more than that.

One of my prize collector's items is a framed poster bestowed upon me by the children at the CP Center. Across the top it reads "Cousin Tuny, Thank you for helping our garden to grow. We love you." Flowers are drawn all over the poster, outlined in green and pink and, in the bloom, the center of each flower, is a little round color picture of the face of each child who attends the Center. The child's name is on a little leaf of the flower. Those are my chosen children in that poster and they give me such inspiration.

I get so many calls from youngsters who are grown and have children of their own. One such call...

"Cuz, you don't know me, and I don't live in Jackson, but you helped raise me. I was three years old and I could say my prayers and my pledge to the flag from watching you on television. I wanted to tell you how much I appreciate it."

That's worth a whole lot. If you can help guide one little life on the road, that's what it's all about.

If I'm angry or frustrated, I can always visit the Cerebral Palsy Center — I leave with a suit of armor and say, 'Come on, world.'

POST HOLE DIGGERS

They put on a big CP telethon in Nashville every year and I went up and appeared with Jayne Mansfield... Her room at the motel was right next to mine and we struck up a conversation. This lady was a PhD and she had a very high IQ.

I asked "Jayne, why is it that you hide behind that sex symbol?"

"Tuny, why do you hide behind those blacked-out teeth and those freckles?"

"Spoken just like a Post Hole Digger — PhD."

She was smart and sharp and had a lot on the stick. We had pictures made together. When we were standin' there, I looked uupp at Jayne with "I hope you don't sneeze 'cause if you come in fresh you'd knock me unconscious!"

She was a good-size woman — 44 in the bust — I'm a 4 too.

All the press were there, everybody watchin' and laughin' at us. I said "In case y'all don't know, that's Jayne Mansfield [up there] and I'm Cousin Tuny [down here]... I didn't want you'all to get us mixed up."

Soon after that appearance, Jayne was killed in a tragic car accident.

In Paducah, Kentucky there were the Crippled Children Telethons. I appeared and performed with Fannie Flagg... she's a hoot and quite a gal, too. We did a mock-up of what used to be

Johnny Carson's Tonight Show... you have to have fun and play around in the midst of the all-night seriousness. You get caught up in your purpose... and the adrenalin is pumping... you forget about the long hours.

The Azalea Festival is an annual event in Wilmington, North Carolina, where my sister Jenny and nephew Bill lived. One year Mitch Miller emceed the star-studded show; I appeared with him and sang several songs with his orchestra.

We were cuttin'-up and Mitch said "You're a real classy dame, you know that? And you're dynamite onstage."

"Thanks a lot. I appreciate that. I just happen to love this crazy business. You ain't no slouch yourself, Cuz!"

Jenny was my chaperone through the weekend of parades and parties. We just had a blast!

Back in the 60's, American Women in Radio and Television graced me with the Golden Mike Award for Outstanding Broadcasting. I was truly honored and looked forward to our national meeting in New York...

Ginger Rogers designed women's lingerie for J.C. Penney and, since J.C. Penney was involved in our meetings that weekend, Ms. Rogers was the special guest. She was booked in the Hilton penthouse and the AWRT members were staying in rooms throughout the hotel.

I had written ahead to see if I could interview Ms. Rogers, and got an appointment with her. When I entered the penthouse, she said "Well, come right on in."

I said "There's something I must do."

"Go ahead and do it."

I sang "'I'm puttin' on my top hat; I'm tyin' up a white tie'... I know everybody's telling you they're a great fan and maybe they are; but nobody has been a bigger fan than me. I've watched all your shows; I've loved to dance all my life; and I've admired you all through the years."

We sat down and they took Polaroid shots of us... the first one that came out didn't have our heads in it. I said "They'll never know who's who, will they?"

I was scheduled to have twenty minutes for the interview; but we got so involved in conversation, I was there about an hour. She told her manager "Leave us alone. We're having too much fun."

Ginger threw a big party, with special invitations, guards, etc. There was a combo playing when she came down these spiral wrought-iron stairs — in hot pink, her favorite color — everything was wound around that, pink everywhere. I was standing at the foot of the stairs and, when she saw me, she started laughing.

I said "You mean you remember 'I'm puttin' on my top hat'?"

"I won't ever forget that performance!"

I had a little gold angel pin sittin' upon my shoulder, and Ginger remarked "I love your little angel."

"That's a Tennessee angel." I took it off and gave it to her.

"Oh, I can't take that."

"I have another one. Please..." I pinned it on her shoulder and she wore it that night.

THE WHITE WIDOWS
"The Barbecue"

Once a year there was this neighborhood to-do at Jim and Anne Avants' house... a real nice affair. It was a take-a-dish deal and b.y.o.b.; they supplied beer and set-ups. Jim was a fine barbecue chef... he had a trailer with all the bbq accountrements and he cooked a whole hog. Everybody gave $2.50 apiece to help pay for the pig. It was an outstanding get-together.

I picked up everybody... had five women in my small car. We looked like sardines... kinda like those clowns... ninety-eleven of 'em comin' out of the little-bitty car in the circus.

We were seated around a table at the barbecue having drinks. Here came Sustuh...

"Ohh, Dawris, it's so wuunderful ta see ya, how-aare-yah?... My-my-myy, what <u>is</u> that on your left ear?"

"It's an ear cuff."

"Whaat, Dawris?? I'm surpriised at you. You <u>know</u> who wears those!"

"Mimi, are you saying that I'm a lesbian?"

"Ohh no, nooo... but you <u>know</u> what <u>they</u> say!"

"I don't give a damn what <u>they</u> say. You don't know what you're talkin' about, 'cause left is right and right is wrong, as far as ear cuffs or earrings are concerned."

I wasn't gonna lose any sleep over it; but, I must say, Sustuh sure does have a way with woorrdds.

And here came Belle with her walker. "Well, how you girls doin'?"

I looked around the table and thought, um-hmm... if a fortune-teller walked up to any of us, she'd say 'Excuse me, may I read your face?'

Belle sits down and Blinker Babcock looks up like, this is my group and my table, what are you doin' sittin' here? Like little girls playing house. Belle keeps lookin' at the doo-dads on the table, little cheese Goldfish and pretzels and stuff.

I said "Come on, Belle, have some."

"Well, I think I will have a few."

"Would you like a drink?"

And Blinker shot her eyes around at me, because it was all her booze... the vodka and the scotch and the bourbon. [This is mine and you can't have any 'cause I didn't invite you to my table... oh me, gonna take my toys and go home] Belle didn't stay very long; she got up and scooted her walker across the lawn.

Mary came back to the table after we went through the buffet line. I said something about drinking vodka and that I still had some of my drink. Mary said "I'm drinking beer."

Blinker piped up, "Where'd you get that beer? Did you bring it with you?"

"No, I got it over there..."

"Well, you've been drinking my scotch. What's the matter? Don't you want any scotch?"

"I just like beer with barbecue."

"Oh well, okay, okay, okay."

Blinker had a bottle of Old Grandad... This cute guy came around the table and Blinker cooed "Hey, you cute thing."

He said "Oh, you're drinkin' Old Grandad."

"Yeah, you want a drink?"

"Yes, I do. I haven't had that in a long time."

He took one drink and spewed "God, this doesn't taste like Old Grandad."

Blinker huffed "Well, that's what it is!"

I got hysterical 'cause Blinker had a habit of getting a Chivas Regal bottle and puttin' Ushers or whatever you call the cheap scotch in it. So there really isn't much tellin' what kind of whiskey was in that Old Grandad bottle. Nice work if you can get it.

This man was helping Jim do all the cooking. He said "Ladies, I'm from Dyersburg, but I work for Mr. Avant at J.C. Bradford."

I said "In what part do you work?"

"I work in commodities — soybeans and pork bellies."

When he left, Etta said "Hell, I know about those commodities. God, we used to buy them commodities by the half-truckload."

I glanced at Mary, and that was it... we broke up laughing and changed the subject...

We were talkin' about a rash of robberies in the neighborhood... it seems that this black man rides a bicycle and breaks in during the day. He goes up to the door, turns the knob... if it's locked, he just takes his shoulder and shoves the door in.

cuz

He ransacks the house and, of course, carts off all kinds of stuff.

Mayola Miller said "You know, Medina, my sister, is just scared being an elderly widow there by herself in her home. She don't even wanna get out and go to church or Sunday School or anything, she's just so scared to get out because of all these robberies. I'm so afraid if she ever gets raped, she'll catch <u>The AIDS</u>."

Mary said she'd better take off and she'd see me at Betsy Madison's tomorrow.

Blinker overheard and asked "What is she having?"

"She's having just a few over for a drink."

"Well, she didn't invite me! Well, I just, well, that's perfectly alright if that's the way she feels about it. I won't ask her to anything else!"

Come to find out later, Blinker called Betsy the next day: "Hi, Bets — I was just thinking about you... I want to share with you my loaf of bread that I brought back from New York. I'd like to bring you three slices. Could I run by around... say... five o'clock?"

[Betsy didn't know that Blinker knew that we knew that who knew]

"Why don't you have a drink with us?"

"Oh? Oh — well... okay/sure/I'd love to."

There's more than one way to get invitations.

As we were all leaving the bbq — Libby, who has the face of a cigar store Indian, stoical — stepped up behind me, tapped me on the shoulder. I turned my head; we were face-to-face. Libby has never told me a joke in all my born life.

Not cracking a smile, she announced "Do you know why the Baptists don't have sex standing up? Because they're afraid somebody will think they're dancing."

Then she walked off.

I almost dropped my teeth.

DIFFERENTLY ABLED / WEST VIRGINIA

I was appointed to the Governor's Committee for the Employment of the Disabled. I call them "differently abled." I was delighted to serve... tryin' to help those folks who can't get around... 'cause there's somethin' they can do. I just thank the Good Lord we don't have to closet them anymore, that they can come out. They are vital human beings who can work and contribute to their communities, like the rest of us... many times, better than the rest of us.

Jean McCoy and I flew to Charleston, West Virginia, where I was to be the celebrity host for a 20-hour telethon for the Cerebral Palsy Association.

On the plane, we were reminiscing and laughing about some of our escapades together — 'frick and frack' — from a talent show that I judged where the gospel, pop, and country-western groups were all the same people... to a country-western show where I performed on a flatbed truck, with all the old men in the audience grabbin' at me... to a fashion show where the mothers and daughters wore twin dresses... and on and on.

There was a driver (as usual, a little old man) waiting to take us to our hotel. He looked like the storekeeper at Hooterville... was retired from driving a bread truck. He decided he was gonna get on the Interstate... got about halfway up the on-ramp and said "Naw, I don't think I wanna do that." He put it into reverse and backed all the way down. I was sitting in the front seat, and I didn't dare look back at Jean... I felt her laughter. I could see the headlines now:

"DORIS FREEMAN AND JEAN McCOY KILLED GOING BACKWARDS ON WEST VIRGINIA ON-RAMP."

I'd appeared in the Charleston area before, for bachelors' auctions — but not with their Cerebral Palsy Telethons. So I took my keyboard with me to rehearsal and plugged that thing right into the band P.A. system. I had worked this out with Karen Boles, the Executive Director of the Cerebral Palsy Association of West Virginia...

I said to the band "Since I'm the celebrity host here, I'm going to do this show like it should be done. So I've written a song here and this is gonna be the theme song." I was just as serious as death. And I broke down on "Everybody Wants My Body But me." They were in the floor when it was over.

"Listen, y'all, I had to do this to break the ice. Now we're gonna get to sink our teeth in and get on with this thing."

We had a good time singing "Gonna Build A Mountain," "God's Special Children," "Jesus Loves Me," "The Sweetest Story Ever Told," "He's My Rock n' Roll Daddy From Dixie, You oughta see him strut his stuff," etc....

It's a very depressed area up there... they have coal mines and everybody's on strike and people are hungry. They do not have a daily Center, as we do. They have services, in that they help get equipment for children, young adults; and help them get to physical therapy. There's the PUTTI project — People United to Teach and Train Individuals — a beautiful situation. They do recycling and these people who have Cerebral Palsy and other problems work there a few hours a week and make a little money... it makes them feel independent, a terrific project. A lot of people are working to get contracts... these kids and parents and friends and family go out and get cans and bottles for recycling. After all, that's the name of the survival game in the 21st Century.

cuz

The poster child, Betty, was an eleven-year-old, cute little redhead in a wheelchair. She was verbal, so I could interview her.

"Betty, tell me about what's been happening to you."

"Cousin Tuny, I just returned from the Shrine Hospital where they operated on my legs again. Guess what? In four or six months, the doctors say that I will probably be able to walk, for the first time in my life. These people helped me get into the hospital and worked it out where they would do the operation up there."

I looked into the camera... "You can't place a price on this."

Your adrenalin comes bubblin' out; I guess you could call that a natural high...

I was seated, making a pitch on camera, when I looked out of the corner of my eye and, on the sidelines, there was a precious little girl standing there; they were kinda holding her up; she was grinning from ear to ear, waving at me — I'd never seen her before in my life. So I just looked over and said "Do you want to come over here with me?"

She said "Uh-huh."

"Come on."

The cameras got the child trying to walk, defying the laws of gravity, little ankles just wobbling... she made it over and hugged my neck.

I said "Do you wanna sit up here beside me?"

"Uh-huh."

She was adorable. "What is your name?"

"My name is Candy."

"That's a good name for you because you're sweeter than candy, I bet."

"My paw-paw says I am."

"How old are you, Candy?"

"I'm four but I'm almost five."

"Ooh, that's a big fistful of fingers."

"Uh-huh. Cousin Tuny, I've been watching you on TV at home."

"You have? That's wonderful."

"I didn't walk till I was three 'cause they operated on my legs, too."

"Well, I know that you're happy you can run around and you can walk. One of these days I bet you'll be out there dancing."

"I hope so."

"Do you have anything else you want to say?"

"I love you."

Here was a child I'd never seen before in my life. That was the top of the mountain.

Before we signed off the air, the Chairman of the Board for the West Virginia Cerebral Palsy Association presented me with a gorgeous plaque... has the outline of the State of West Virginia, my name, and "Thank you for helping us grow in 19-9-0." It's one of the prettiest things I've ever seen.

Getting back to the airport, with our trusty little driver, was even more of an experience than arriving and backing down the on-ramp.

He was a sweetheart of a guy, but hit with the ugly stick so bad, as the old sayin' goes, he has to whip his bottom to get it in bed with his face every night.

He kinda squealed, in a high-pitched tone... "Cousin Tuny, I've been watchin' you on television all weekend. This just thrills me ta no end, I swear! I told the wife, I said 'Wife, I sure would like to talk to her, but she prob'ly won't talk to me.'"

"Don't be silly... we'll talk all the way to the airport."

And <u>he</u> did — 90 miles a minute. I hardly got a word in edgewise. He could talk the legs off a billy goat.

Got to the airport — our flight was cancelled. I swanee, we ended up flying all over the northeast, midwest and southeast, in and out of airports, for hours and hours, to get back to Memphis, to take the little 'weed eater' into Jackson. And I wasn't even driving.

CARL PERKINS-"KING OF ROCKABILLY"

"Circles of Hope"

Carl saw a picture of a child who died from abuse. He thought of how much the youngster resembled his own son... and our legendary rockabilly artist vowed to help however he could to see that other children in West Tennessee would not suffer from abuse. That promise led to a partnership with the

Jackson Exchange Club, in creating what is now the Exchange Club/Carl Perkins Center for the Prevention of Child Abuse.

The Center works with families to break the cycle of child abuse. More parents are seeking help, and the Center is establishing offices in surrounding counties... There is family counseling, a parent training lab; caseworkers make weekly checks on families where children have suffered abuse. The Center also offers crisis intervention for children in danger, emergency food, clothing and medical care funds.

The child abuse "Circle of Hope" Telethon was born in 1981 and continues surviving every August. I co-hosted with Carl until his untimely death in 1998... and, like the Cerebral Palsy Telethon, we broadcast live over WBBJ-TV. We have gospel groups, videos from the Oak Ridge Boys, Larry Gatlin, Kenny Rogers... Carl Perkins' son and Prince of Rock-a-billy, Stan Perkins, Rusty Mac, Wes Henley, Chuck McGill, Paula Bridges, Rita McCaslin, and our wonderful, dedicated local talent.

In my Tuny dress [we finally used all the feed out of the sack], with matching seat covers [I no longer black out my teeth — I've 'grown up'], I warble a few tunes and we talk to the good souls about caring and sharing. Naturally Carl would perform with his guitar. The contentment and self-esteem in giving to the health and happiness of these children is like no other feeling in the world. This is a ticket to ride... you really feel like you've earned your salt when you contribute to the welfare of stricken human beings who are the future of this country.

When we ring the doorbell of someone's heart and they ring us back, it's powerful. "Mama an' them and all the li'l goats are proud of you. Count your blessings and pass 'em on." We carry on...

We build "Circles of Hope" for abused boys and girls when folks call in with a pledge from their hearts. And we all do it together... as I sing with the precious children in need of help... Side By Side.

Oh, we ain't got a barrel of money
Maybe we're ragged and funny
But we'll travel along
Singin' a song
Side by side

We don't know what's comin' tomorrow
Maybe it's trouble and sorrow
But we'll carry our road
Sharin' our load
Side by side

In all kinds of weather
What if the sky should fall
As long as we're together
It doesn't matter at all

We'll keep this love here forever
No matter what be the weather
And we'll travel along
Singin' a song
Side by side

cuz

The Heart Association held a celebration/dinner for me on my birthday one year. They raised several thousand dollars for the Heart Fund, and that was the most important thing. It was a lovely affair, like "This Is Your Life" presentation. Full of surprises and crazy goings-on. The Mayor, County Commissioner and Governor gave me awards, 'Outstanding Tennessean.' Fortunately, two of my children, daughter-in-law and grandsons were able to make it.

The finest compliment came from Carl Perkins. He wrote and sang with his guitar:

Some folks say — oh, it will get done —

they'll find someone to help

But there are a few who say — step back,

I'll do it myself

We've all been blessed to know that one —

even though they're few

A Lady loaded down with love —

Cousin Tuny, that's you

How do you talk about Tuny, there's just

no place to start —

They come few and far between, with her

kinda love and heart

She's our special Lady — Jackson's gift

from God —

She never says no to helping out —
especially where kids are involved
We all know about the CP Center —

I sure know about the child abuse
Whenever any of us need help for anything —
Cousin Tuny, we call on you
So thank you, Cuz, for all you do —
now I'd like to say —
I think you really are pleasing God
And, oh yes, Happy Birthday
Hope you have many many more —
May your good dreams all come true
By the way, I took a while to say —
Tuny, I love you

The life of love you're living now
Would make a beautiful song —
May your soul be already safe in Heaven
Before the devil knows you're gone —
So thank you, sweetheart —
thanks again for all the things you do —
We're all proud of our city of Jackson —
And, Tuny, we're especially proud of you
God Bless You!

cuz

Gee, I feel unworthy to have such a tribute from this great guy. Carl had a heart as big as all outdoors. He was a sweet, sweet man...

THE WHITE WIDOWS

"Hongry"

The swingin' geriatric bunch were having a drink at the Club, when Libby started talkin' about the Daughters of the American Revolution and her committee meetings...

"Tuny, have you ever looked into your background?"

"God, it'd scare the hell out of me if I did. I expect my ancestors swung by their tails from the trees."

"Well now, Tuny, you oughta look that up 'cause you're probably one of the Daughters of the American Revolution."

"Why, my ancestors probably started the Revolution."

I don't care about that stuff. It may be important to a point, but what's that have to do with the price of oats? It's what's happening today! Those annals are written in history, and that's fine; so be it.

All these doo-dad committees and ways and means committees... oh now... 'we'll please call this meeting to order.' It just bores me. When you're up past your elbows to your earlobes in focus groups and committees and extracurricular to-do's, it gets difficult to remember the objective. Sometimes you have to roll up your britches legs, it gets so deep.

I had run into Claudine the day before at the grocery store. She'd said this was the fourth stop in her search for a bargain on asparagus, and this was the cheapest... so far.

"Claudine, that's one gorgeous automobile you were

driving yesterday."

"Oh, that's my divorce present to myself. When I left Beau, I just walked out and didn't ask him for <u>anything</u>! And I didn't even know how to write a check!"

I got my tongue hung around my eye tooth and thought, I wouldn't tell anybody I was that dumb.

"Do you know what I did? Well, I just went down to celebrate and bought myself a Lincoln Continental! I've always had smaller cars before, I drove convertibles. And, by the way, I've had car dealers tell me, 'I'll give you a new car and a hundred dollars for your car.'"

I sat there and thought, Everybody who believes that, stand on your head naked on Court Square.

"And you know what else? Paid cash for it. Just did!! And I told my children, I said 'I have enough money to send you to any college you want to go to. I'll lift you up, but you've got to study'"..............

As Claudine went on and on, I sorta beamed-out and reflected back to singing at the VFW on Sunday nights years ago with Jimmy Allen playing piano. They paid me 15 dollars for it, and I could use the 15 dollars... hoping to get home safe all those many, many nights that I was out on the road dodging drunks from band dates... then I'd tape radio commercials and airmail them to the East Coast on weekends. Dixie Carter's father ran a store in Huntingdon and gave me toys one Christmas that made Santa Claus possible. I didn't work from 9 to 5. I worked from can to can't — I had to. For the last several years my ex-husband Jimmy has been very generous to our children and I appreciate that. However, I have, at times, felt like I was so low I could look up and see the belly of a snake.

I said "Claudine, you ought to get on your hands and knees

and thank God that you had some money."

She didn't hear a word I said.

"Well, I know, but you know I had never done anything much."

Well, she still hasn't done anything much.

"What are you doing now?"

"You know, my column."

"What column?"

"Oh, I write for the <u>Goochville Gazette</u>."

Whoopdedoo. That's about four plateaus under <u>Grit</u>, a former weekly paper that cost a nickel, rural almanac type of information, with recipes, etc.

"I try to birdbrain the news."

I thought, that isn't hard for you to do.

"Mimi [Sustuh] said 'Claudine, you just don't know how to take a man when you leave him.'"

I said "Naw, you sure don't because Mimi took Philip for everything." But that's Sustuh.

Claudine looked at me so funny. Mary was falling in her plate, hysterical. I was amused... you'd have thought that she walked out starvin' to death.

"Claudine, have you ever been hungry?"

"Oh yes."

"Have you ever been hongry? You know the difference?"

"I don't guess I do."

"There's hungry, hungrier, hungriest and hongry. I've been hongry. I don't think you've really attained a genuine sense of value until you've been hongry."

Am I having fun yet? Why am I here?

Geeminy Christmas. Age is a state of mind, and most of these cats are real sharp; they do think young. But they are in another world.

I'll stay where I am, as I am.

God love the little old rich people.

cuz

RETREADING

Doris Freeman retired. Cousin Tuny is retreading.

    I was privileged to volunteer at Jackson-Madison County General Hospital for more than 25 years before becoming Director of Marketing and Public Relations. I believe the hospital is where I was meant to end my career, and they were some of the most rewarding years of my life. My work was exciting and I've been happy to be just a little part of the miracles that happen there every day. Those health care workers are the best in the world — I sure will miss 'em.

    The hospital has about 50 Department Directors, Administrative Staff... I was at a Department Directors meeting when Jimmy King, whose daughters went to school with my oldest daughters, was introduced as a special guest. I was totally surprised when he presented me with the Elks Lodge Distinguished Citizenship Award. It was lovely, a real nice thing to happen.

    At my retirement party, my fabulous staff just outdid themselves... great food, family, many friends I've known forever, presents, and a funny yet touching poem written by Rosemary Mestan and signed by all the right hands who made our department a success.

    Bill Holland and Richard Gilliam are florists... They decorated the glass front of their shop with a massive white heart that read "I Love Tuny" in red letters... blown up 'Cuz' photos surrounding a Tuny-dressed mannequin. When I saw it, I told

Bill and Richard — "You suppose I passed away and they forgot to tell me?"

Speaking of which, it seemed like an appropriate time to have a physical examination. I made an appointment with my gynecologist, Dr. Don Lewis — OBGYN: 'Oh Boy, Got Ya Now'

After he did all the pokin' and punchin' and feelin' and fumblin' and thumbin' and jazz, Don said "Tuny, you're gonna live forever."

"That's because neither side wants me, no place for me to go."

Of course, anything can happen — cancer, strokes, heart attacks, etc., we don't make those choices. But I'm gonna run from fast and try to prevent 'em as much as I can.

He said "One of the reasons you're in such great shape is your outlook on life, and the fact that you've worked hard."

"You know, work is the greatest therapy in the world. You get your mind cleaned out and get your heart cleaned out and connect the two, that's all you have to worry about really... and the greatest treasure in the world is peace of mind, and I'm gonna have that if I have to eat a pea and a cracker a day. But you know what's eating this world alive, Don? It's this plague, it's an epidemic."

"What are you talking about?"

"Osteorectalymelitis... don't you know what that is?"

"Well, no."

"Are you tellin' me, you're a fine gynecologist, and you do not know what that means? That is the nerve at the end of your backbone, at your tailbone, that comes straight up your backbone and up the back of your neck, comes out through your eyes and gives you a crappy outlook on life."

He roared... "Oh God, how right you are."

That's a Tuny diagnosis, a Tunyism.

I was happier than I've ever been in my life because the most glorious thing about retiring was having time to spend with the most wonderful man in my life, Bill (W.C.) Harris. When we started dating, I was at the ripe young age of 65... not a point in time when you expect to be smitten. We had known each other for years, as I've mentioned, but not like this. It was really fantastic.

We went to Bill's 50th class reunion at the University of Tennessee in Knoxville and I struck up a conversation with a couple...

"How many children do you have?"

The wife said "We have four. How many do you'all have?"

"Between us, we have six."

"Oh, how long have you been married?"

"We aren't married. We just fool around. And someday we're gonna have a meeting with the children."

"Oh, oh, well, well, well... Excuse me, I see someone over there I need to speak to."

When I was interviewed about my retirement, there were the usual questions... "What are your plans?"...

"If the mood strikes me, that's how I'm livin'...

Tuny will continue entertaining —

Doris is going to rest until the baby comes."

EPILOGUE

Just Me — Bein' Doris

'Cuz' is a term I've used when greeting people for as long as I can remember. Now it comes in handy when I'm about as sharp as a boll of cotton and can't remember a name... I can just say "This is my cuz and I want you to meet my other cuz"... blame it on Medicare, now that I'm getting my shampoo mixed up with the orange Kool-Aid. When you've been around the world twice, once on a bicycle... it ain't easy to pedal that bicycle across those oceans, especially if you don't have a ten-speed or a motor on the little dude.

Whenever I get a hitch in my git-along that makes my feel-bad hurt worse, I can sit down in my little sitting room and look around... It helps me get my act together and set my priorities. That's how I do it, because I remember... I glance around at the picture of little John with me and Santa, past all the pictures of the children at the Cerebral Palsy Center, the pictures of my children, grandsons, and I look at the plaques from the Cancer Society, the Heart Fund and Heart Association, the Cerebral Palsy Center, Prevention of Child Abuse, United Negro College Fund, Chamber of Commerce... I wouldn't take anything for these remembrances... not for a farm in Georgia... they all mean something to me...

The Chamber of Commerce always makes me smile... they once gave me a waxpaper bikini and reservations to the Riviera. All I had to do was pick up the trip's tab... the JayCees held a "Cousin Tuny Day" event and we made a little money for the CP Center. They roasted me, the "mouth of the South," but I sat in a tub of cold water and got in the last word... fun, fun, fun!

Someone remarked to me "You have so many plaques and 'Honorary' this and 'Honorary' that"... I said "Yeah, and each one is a different treasure." I love being an Honorary Deputy Sheriff... qualifying with a pistol, I do pretty good. If we were in a disaster, they could call on us to help... but I don't think they'd take me out on a posse, not the way I ride a horse.

I tell a lot of people I have four fabulous children, two in show business and two that are normal... Pat, Cindie, Jim, and Connie. Jim traded signed postcards of me and Cindie for baseball cards... and, throughout her travels, Cindie is asked "Excuse me, is your mother Cousin Tuny?" These are people who were on my TV show when Cindie was a little girl performing with me. She says the capper came when she thought she was alone in the clouds on the sun pyramid in Mexico City... Cindie heard a gentle Southern accent... "Excuse me..." She turned around and smiled — "Yes, she is."

I suppose I was a shuffler of seconds, as Jim is wont to say... I always tried to think of the big umbrella and we all worked together. An "I can't do that" attitude gives me pains I can't locate. We can and we did. We were never bored, that's for sure. In making decisions, I had to have a system. I take a piece of paper and draw a line down the middle. I write down the positive aspects on one side and the negative points on the other. Then I place the paper under my pillow and forget it until the next day. Works for me, as they say.

I look at my four grandsons and my gorgeous great-grandson and think about their running and playing... I see so many who cannot... and so many parents who would give anything if their children could get up out of those wheelchairs and run and holler and get into things like normal little boys do. We have a lot to be thankful for.

Seems like I spend a lot of time going to the funeral home —

that's my vintage hangin' out again. It's stressful, you know, stress is when your body sweats bullets and your mind shoots blanks. When my time comes to try to pass my harp audition on high for The Man Upstairs, I don't want a lot of moaning and groaning, because I've shoved more living into the years I've been on this earth than five or six average folks. I haven't missed much and I never intend to get old. I guess if I had my life to live over again, I don't know that I'd change it very much. I'd probably make it a bigger mess the second time around.

I don't know how many more years I'll be able to kick my heels up this high. I can tell each year that my snapper-backer loses a little more elasticity... I don't snap back quite as fast as I used to, but I've got a lot of mileage on this model... so far it's holding up fairly well.

I think you just have to hang in there by your fingernails, and sometimes you think you're on the end of the limb and somebody sawed it in half and you can hear it poppin' every few minutes, it's gonna come loose... As Agnes used to say, they can't eat you, you're too salty.

One of my favorite quotes that I find excellent, is by George Bernard Shaw: "Life is not just a little candle to me, it's a great big torch and I want to make it as bright as possible before I pass it on to future generations." I think everybody needs to take those words to heart.

I feel like I'm one of the richest people in the world. I have four magnificent children, the greatest treasures of my life, four fine grandsons, a beautiful great-grandson, and I've experienced true love... Bill Harris was a God-Sent Blessing. At 65, I was living a fairy tale love life. Bill kept saying, "Tuny, we're making memories." I was on Cloud Nine, and then — February, 1996 — that beautiful life came to a screeching halt. We were aboard the Royal Princess on our way to Panama Canal.

As we were docking on the island of Curacoa, Bill suffered a massive stroke. We had to leave the ship — and the love of my life died on that island. I thank God for getting us together and giving us five and a half years of a wonderful, exciting, sublime storybook life.

We lived fast, loved hard, laughed often, and made beautiful memories... YESSIRREEBOBOLINKO!

AND THAT'S A WRAP

INDEX

Foreword- Stan Perkins	9
Prologue- "Pritchett"	11
Mattie Branch	15
War of the Worlds	25
Dixie Aroma	26
Getting Out	28
Birth Control & All My Other Children	30
To Dye For	34
The Birth of "Cousin Tuny"	36
The Cousin Tuny Show	38
The Dixie Rebel Band	47
Ted Mack & the Wasp Attack	51
The Moonglows	57
Miss Hatchie Bottom	60
All the Other Children	69
Dianne and Mark	73
Minnie Pearl	77
Ruth	80
Mortgaged Plymouth	87

Vicks Salve	95
Miss Teola	97
Hello Dolly	101
Symphonically Yours	105
John	107
Agnes- Letting Go	112
Jenny	118
Christmastime	121
Santa	124
Mr. Colie / Uncle Charlie	128
Just Cuz- Bein' Tuny	131
Off The Air & Into the Fray	133
Woman of the Year	135
Photographs	138
Horses and Me	152
Dogs and Me	156
Female Chauvinist Pigs	158
Just Cuz- Bein' Tuny	160
Jim Ray	161
Gold Medal / Camp Bluebird	167
North and South	170
Begin the Bidet	173

Code Penal	174
Tuckus	176
Just Cuz- Bein' Tuny	178
Sam Siegel	180
Ode to Gertrude	185
The Little Meeting	189
Just Cuz- Bein' Tuny	191
Body Parts	192
The White Widows- "The Wedding"	194
Louise	197
Just Cuz- Bein' Tuny	201
The White Widows- "Aw, Shucks"	202
Some Good Gore	205
Full Chicken Colonel	210
Spaced Out	214
The American Flag	217
Beauty Is Deep	222
My Man	227
Just Cuz- Bein' Tuny	229
The White Widows- "Sustuh"	231
Making Right	233
1,000 Points of Light	235

The Cerebral Palsy Center "God's Special Children"	237
Post Hole Diggers	250
The White Widows- "The Barbecue"	253
Differently Abled / West Virginia	258
Carl Perkins- "Circles of Hope"	263
The White Widows- "Hongry"	270
Retreading	274
Epilogue- "Just Me – Bein' Doris"	278

CUZ

A Note About the Co-Author

Cindie Haynie owns and operates, "Stereotypists" in Hollywood, California. She is an actress, and Tuny's daughter.

A note from Tuny: "Without Cindie, this book would not have been possible."

"Doris is one of a kind in this day and age. We need more like her in our world. She truly loves people, especially children; and she gives of herself so unselfishly.

I consider her to be a "Tennessee Treasure." I am so thankful to have had the opportunity to be her friend. ... I could probably write a book on all the wonderful experiences we have shared and I treasure each one."

~ Jean McCoy

"First, you must understand that Doris is a complicated personality. Behind that hillbilly "good, country girl look" is an astute business woman, a person who knows exactly what she is doing every minute and a consummate showman.

The 'Cousin Tuney Show' was more than a TV show. It was a decade long chronicle of Jackson Madison County history. We will always remember Doris' words - 'Do you want to entertain or be entertained.'

Tuny will always be my friend. Her love of people will endure long after the songs and jokes are gone. The title of this book should be, 'Nice Guys Finish First.' In Tuny's own words- 'That's what it is all about.' "

~ Jim Hoppers, Former Program Director of WDXI-TV

Cuz Tuny is one of the rare jewels God puts on this earth to teach us how to live life to the fullest. Her life has been full of laughter, tears, some setbacks, but always love. Through out her life, she has taught us how to love and care for all God's children. Because of her labor of love, there are children all over West Tennessee who have lived better lives. Thank you Cuz for being a part of our world - we love you.

~ dn english, Publisher
Main Street Publishing